SOCIAL CONTROL OF THE WELFARE STATE

SOCIAL CONTROL OF THE WELFARE STATE

Morris Janowitz

THE UNIVERSITY OF CHICAGO PRESS
Chicago and London

The University of Chicago Press, Chicago 60637
The University of Chicago Press, Ltd., London

©1976 by Elsevier Scientific Publishing Co., Inc.
All rights reserved. Published 1976 by Elsevier Scientific
Publishing Co., Inc. Phoenix Edition 1977
Printed in the United States of America

81 80 79 78 77 54321

ISBN: 0-226-39308-9
LC: 77-79911

Published by arrangement with Elsevier North-Holland, Inc.

Contents

Tables

Preface

This sociological essay is a reflection of my long-term interest in the old-fashioned concept of "social control." As such, it is a fragment of an ongoing study of the transformation of United States society over the last half century. No doubt to use the term "social control" is to run the risk of being misinterpreted. In its classical sense, as formulated by the pioneer sociologists at the turn of the century, "social control" did not mean conformity—and certainly not social repression. Instead, it was defined as "self-regulation" and as the capacity of a society or social group to pursue a set of higher moral values.

Social control was and must still be seen as the obverse of coercive control. Elsewhere I have traced the intellectual history of this sociological concept.[1] One must either use the notion of social control or invent an equivalent term if one is to confront the profound predicaments of the contemporary welfare state under parliamentary rule.

My concern is with the quality and effectiveness of mass welfare institutions and their political consequences in advanced industrialized societies that have

---

[1]Morris Janowitz, "Social Control and Sociological Theory," *American Journal of Sociology*, LXXXI (July 1975): 82-108.

competitive election systems. All advanced industrialized nations have displayed a long-term growth in expenditures for social welfare. Moreover, this growth has been most rapid since the end of World War II. But I believe that it is necessary to go beyond the assertion that the expansion of the welfare expenditures is a "universal" characteristic of industrialized nations. The welfare state in my terms is more than a prescribed level of welfare expenditures. Moral and political issues are involved. The welfare state, as explored in this essay, has two central characteristics. First, the ideological, political, and moral justification of welfare expenditures is that the state can intervene in the management of the economic system in order to assist each household and each person to pursue goals of their own choosing. Of course, welfare expenditures can and have been justified for national and for authoritarian goals. Second, to achieve the moral goals of the welfare state, parliamentary institutions are required to guide the scope, priorities, and effect of welfare expenditures. There must also be auxiliary institutions of mass representation at the local level to ensure that the welfare agencies perform effectively and responsibly.

Thus, I am interested in particular in the influence of the welfare state over the last three decades on the political parties and on the political behavior of the citizenry. This is an analogous issue to the long-term effect of military expenditures on parliamentary regimes. My focus is mainly on the United States, with limited observations about other Western nations. Throughout Western parliamentary systems, the growth of the welfare state has been accompanied by the emergence of weak political regimes governing by narrow margins or by unstable coalitions or even as minority governments. This is hardly to deny the crucial social advances that have been wrought by increased welfare expenditures. However, the issue at hand is that of explaining how the growth of the welfare state has contributed to the development of such regimes. My underlying assumption is that the contemporary format of welfare institutions has made its contribution to the "crisis" of political legitimacy. The procedure of analysis is to make use of the notion of social control. The logic of the argument rests on examining the manner in which the political economy of the welfare state has transformed, or at least modified, the social structure in a nation such as the United States and then to trace out the consequences of these changes on popular political participation.

My approach is that of the sociologist. This essay derives from the observation that sociology from its very origins and in its persistent perspectives has been based on the assertion that marketplace economics and exchanges did not and could not account for the existence of the social order. The study of the modern nation-state requires a focus on welfare institutions, since welfare institutions make the existence of the social order possible and simultaneously create particular predicaments that political regimes encounter. The enlargement of welfare expenditures serves only to complicate the tasks of political control and management.

It has become fashionable—in fact, almost

required—for social scientists to state their values and preferences as they present their analysis of contemporary institutions. One cannot object, although often I wonder how helpful such pronouncements are in the advancement of sociological scholarship. Frequently the testament is obvious and at times highly ritualized. Perhaps this is justified because sociologists have acquired multiple audiences and may have readers who are not familiar with them as citizens. In any case, "welfare" has become a particularly controversial issue, so that the implications of research can easily be distorted. Thus it has become indispensable to indicate the "ideological" perspective one holds on the problems of the welfare state.

These underlying issues of the relations between social research, social values, and public policy were raised in the 1930s by writers such as Karl Mannheim, Harold Lasswell, and Robert Lynd.[2] I do not believe that there has been impressive intellectual progress in formulating or resolving them, although the intensity of the debate has greatly increased. In fact, I must assert that I am still committed to the belief in a "value-free" sociology—as Max Weber meant and not as vulgarized in contemporary debate.[3] I believe that

---

[2]Karl Mannheim, *Man and Society in an Age of Reconstruction* (London: Kegal Paul, 1940); Harold Lasswell, *Democracy through Public Opinion* (Menasha, Wis.: George Banta, 1941); Robert S. Lynd, *Knowledge for What? The Place of Social Science in American Culture* (Princeton, N.J.: Princeton University Press, 1939).

[3]Max Weber, "Der Sinn der 'Wertfreiheit' der soziologischen und ökonomischen Wissenschaften," *Logos,* II (1917). See also Max Weber, *On the Methodology of the Social Sciences*, trans. Edward A. Shils and Henry A. Finch (Glencoe, Ill.: The Free Press, 1949); Max Weber, *On Universities*, trans. Edward A. Shils (Chicago: University of Chicago Press, 1974).

there is a meaningful difference between a fact and a statement of preference and that the search for objective description and analysis of social reality is a legitimate if most difficult enterprise. To Max Weber, "value-free" social science was linked to academic freedom since he believed that social research should be free of the values of the Prussian state bureaucracy that controlled the university system.[4] Of course, group interest impinges on and threatens to distort the observation of social reality. But even more important, every statement of fact threatens the interest of some social group, so vested interests erect strong barriers to social research. But we cannot get caught in an infinite regression. Social research is a collective and professional enterprise, and it can and does make progress by means of its own norms of consensual validity. It remains a system of control by colleagues because sociologists have a significant degree of group autonomy.

The task is full of ambiguities, but workable solutions and resolutions are possible. To overcome distortions, the social scientist must pursue sociology as a group enterprise with professional standards. Social scientists must act responsibly in the collection and dissemination of their information. And most important, social scientists must recognize that personal and social values can enhance the vitality of research. They can, in fact, introduce the goal of maximizing specific values into their research as a highly productive intellectual strategy. The essential issues are a

---

[4]See Lewis A. Coser, "Max Weber, 1864–1920," *Masters of Sociological Thought* (New York: Harcourt Brace, 1971), pp. 217–260.

high degree of self-awareness on the part of the social scientist and effective mechanisms of critical review of research findings.

Thus, I think of myself, and have over a lifetime thought of myself, as a social democrat—fully aware of the imprecision of the category. I believe that the state—and voluntary associations—can and must organize a system of welfare in order to assist individuals to realize their personal goals, their dignity, and their self-esteem. At the same time, a social democracy rests on the operation of an effective competitive electoral system, which requires voluntary associations and individual initiative that have a viable existence outside of the governmental process. Therefore, there is a point at which the extension of the state weakens the viability of the competitive parliamentary regime; as a result, there are limits to the enlargement of the welfare system. This possibility has been traditionally recognized by philosophers of social democracy. The new difficulty that has developed since 1945 is the emergence of weak political regimes unable to establish decisively public priorities. The implications of such institutional trends are disruptive of the values and goals of social democracy. Concretely, the 1970s will require increases in public expenditures for welfare. However, the expenditures hardly require confiscatory tax increases, although tax reform is a high-priority requirement. Moreover, the decade will require extensive institution building in welfare as well if the quality of welfare is to be improved and political predicaments are to be resolved.

In this monograph, the strategy of my analysis—or

rather my aspirations—has been first to outline the ideological, normative, and symbolic appeals that have accompanied and facilitated the emergence of the welfare state in the United States.

Second, I am concerned with the institutional growth of the welfare state—its institutional base—in the United States. The enlargement of the welfare state has not been a gradual evolution but has been linked to particular historical events, which have acted as political thresholds—in particular, the Great Depression and, even more so, World War I and World War II. If the growth of the welfare state is a reflection of the increased economic product of industrialism, the forms and character of welfare—the quality and meaning of welfare services—reflect both the normative context and the institutional history of each Western nation-state.

Third, it is necessary to explore the contemporary political economy of the welfare state. The tensions and strains of a capitalist nation have been attributed to its economic surplus and economic profit. The inability to make use effectively of its economic profit leads to social misery, depressions, and imperialist wars, it is argued. The contrary assumption seems more pertinent. Societal trends and the process of bargaining politics have produced a "permanent" system of deficit government spending. Whether one uses a fiscalist or a monetarist point of view or both, chronic inflation and persistent high levels of unemployment have come to be called by economists "stagflation." The increase in the demand for social welfare without the effective allocation of economic resources makes the political management of the welfare state very difficult and in effect distorts its fundamental goals.

Thus, fourth, it is necessary to examine the consequences the welfare state has on the social structure and the system of social stratification. My argument is that the welfare state has fundamentally altered the social structure and thereby transformed and strained the system of social control. The social position of each household and each person does not rest only on its and his or her positions in the occupational system. It has come to involve each person's links to and claims on the welfare system—the new "equities" that the welfare system has created.

The economic claims and transfers of social welfare have been designed to redistribute income, and they have made a limited contribution in this direction. In their absence, the social conditions of an advanced industrial society would be intolerable. However, the influence of social welfare clearly extends in a significant and pervasive fashion upward through the social structure. Social welfare benefits are in their own right essential for wide segments of the middle class.

Fifth, my analysis seeks to examine the political effects of a system of stratification and inequality resulting from the admixture of occupational position and the accrual of welfare benefits. The contemporary social structure makes it more difficult and more complex for citizens to calculate their political self-interest. The result is the transformation of traditional stable linkages between socioeconomic groupings and political affiliation. The electorate is more and more characterized by high degrees of volatility in political preference and self-conceptions and by fragmentation of political choice. The result is that political parties are less and less able to generate clear-cut political majorities that would give them effective power in the executive and legislative arenas. In short, the accomplishments of the welfare state are one source of the political fragmentation and political stalemate.

The final sections of this monograph seek to explore the issue of institution building required for the reconstruction of social welfare and for more effective social control. Of necessity, this task rests on exploring alternative mechanisms for determining economic allocations for social welfare. Likewise, it is necessary to formulate alternative models of social welfare institutions that are explicitly designed to overcome the high and excessive levels of fragmentation that characterize the contemporary agencies of social welfare. But any effort at institution building for social welfare must return to the psychological foundations of welfare and assess whether a materialistic hedonism and a consumer-oriented format of social welfare can implement the transcendental goals of the welfare state. In a political democracy these goals are concerned with the intrinsic value of each human being regardless of his or her income productivity. The central thrust in the direction of institution building rests on new forms of citizen participation at all levels of decision making, but citizen participation that is realistically related to the tasks to be performed. There can be no avoidance of the political reality that periodic national elections serve as the key regulating mechanisms of social and political control. Therefore, the task of institution building is to develop new modes of citizen participation—especially extraelectoral participation—that will enhance the effectiveness and legitimacy of the basic mechanism of self-regulation, namely the national electoral process.

Social scientists have erroneously assumed the task of "futurologists" and therefore are prone to estimate the chances of "survival" or "collapse" of our contemporary social and political institutions. If such speculations serve to clarify contemporary society, they have an intellectual point, although I have strong resistance to such endeavors. Much of these efforts is captured by mechanical theories of history. Of course, I write this analysis because I believe that parliamentary regimes remain viable enough to effect their own adaptation without first having to face the disruption of a fundamental breakdown. However, of course, the possibility exists that either gradually or more suddenly our society could move toward more authoritarian systems of economic allocation and political decision making, which, although it would incorporate the symbols and central practices of social welfare, would in effect emerge as "rightist" authoritarianism—authoritarianism in the American vein with pervasive overtones of populism.

But if one practices the doubtful art of sociological futurology, success and failure are not the only two outcomes. Logically and actually there is the third outcome—no outcome—a continuation of current and chronic tensions and dissatisfactions. The idea of drastic transformation of contemporary industrial society is in part the view that a modern society, because of its high technology, is easily vulnerable to pressures of disruption. The breakdown of a single electrical switching station, even for a few hours, immobilizes the population of a whole region. The inability of a state legislature to regulate malpractice suits produces endless turmoil in the major hospitals. In this view, the accumulation of such tensions undermines the basic institutions of modern society.

By contrast, the peasant society—the society that has come to be called the traditional society—can tolerate much higher levels of disarticulation. It could be the case that such a theory of history is incomplete and in fact misleading. In the peasant society, political crises might well have left the bulk of the society untouched, since most political crises were unrelated to the central concerns of the peasantry. But a specific change in the ecology or a specific medical problem could produce widespread misery and destruction because there were no alternative mechanisms for dealing with the food supply and no alternative institutional resources.

An advanced industrial society has the advantage that its complex division of labor enables it to develop and to utilize alternative modes of response—both to minor and to major crises. The intellectual view of political crisis in Western society is that of tension leading to dramatic and drastic transformation of the political arrangements. Such an eventuality cannot be ruled out as the consequence of the contemporary dilemmas of the "new economics" and the difficulties of transforming the welfare state. But the imagery of drastic, extensive, and radical transformations as they have occurred in the last 150 years in the West may give way to a new state of chronic tension, to partial solution and enormous acceptance of sociopolitical strain, to institutionalized "demi-crisis" and "non-solution." In this regard, my thinking converges with the point of view set forth by Barrington Moore, Jr., in his essay "Reflections on the Causes of Human Misery and upon Certain Proposals to Eliminate Them."[5] It is not a pleasant prospect, but at least the recognition of this eventuality should serve to mobilize intellectual and political resources for the long haul.

---

[5] Barrington Moore, Jr., *Reflections on the Causes of Human Misery and upon Certain Proposals to Eliminate Them* (Boston: Beacon Press, 1972).

The Dilemmas
of the Welfare State

I:

One does not have to be doctrinaire to recognize the profound dilemmas confronting the welfare state. Even the strongest advocates of welfare will attest to its failure to eliminate poverty. Its strongest critics will contend that it has been accompanied by a persistence and even an escalation of domestic sociopolitical conflict rather than the increase in consensus that it was supposed to achieve. On a very pragmatic basis, the welfare state has been accompanied by disruptive political struggles over the appropriate level of expenditure for welfare and by unresolved debate about the fraction of the gross national product required for capital investments to sustain economic growth.

Of course, it is possible to speak of the difficulties of the welfare state under advanced industrialism in economic terms. Since 1970, the growth of the welfare system has been accompanied by both high levels of inflation and chronic unemployment. We speak of real unemployment, not measured unemployment. The key indicator of inflation has been added to that of unemployment. Inflation in and of itself creates new forms of social tension and human misery; it also introduces pervasive elements of uncertainty in the out-look of most of the citizenry. The combination of un-employment and a high level of inflation underlies the inability of the political institutions under the welfare state to resolve economic and social conflict. The new economic condition of stagflation raises the prospect of very low rates of economic growth—rates that strain and limit the aspirations of the welfare state.

Although the roots of the welfare state push far back in history, its extensive growth and its resulting di-lemmas, for the purposes of this essay, are encom-passed by the period 1945 to 1975 in Western Euro-pean parliamentary democracies, the United States, Canada, Australia, and New Zealand. Below the nor-mative and institutional dimensions of the welfare state are set forth. At this point the "welfare state" refers to government practices of allocating at least 8 to 10 percent of the gross national product to welfare. The definition of welfare includes all public expendi-tures for health, education, income maintenance, de-ferred income and funds for community development, including housing allocations.

In quantitative terms, the United States has lagged behind as compared with selected major industrialized nations. By 1935, welfare expenditures had reached close to 10 percent of the gross national product. The figure dropped to a low point of 4.4 percent during World War II and returned to 10 percent by 1966. On a comparative cross-national basis, the United States has expanded its welfare expenditures more slowly than other major Western European nations, but the gap has been closing. By 1970, welfare expenditures in the Federal Republic of West Germany had reached 19.5 percent of the gross national product, in France, 20.9 percent, while the comparable figure for the United States was 15.3 percent, reaching 17.0 percent in 1971.[1] Since 1971 the gap has continued to close.

The welfare state and welfare expenditures are not synonymous. The welfare state rests on the political assumption that the well-being of its citizens is enhanced not only by allocations derived from their occupations and the marketplace but also from grants regulated by the central government. It is necessary to point out that the welfare state involves at least two additional elements. First, under the welfare state, the extent and nature of welfare expenditures are conditioned decisively by parliamentary regimes, that is, they reflect political demands and consent and not authoritarian decisions. Second, it is accepted as a legitimate goal of the political system to intervene through governmental institutions in order to create the conditions under which its citizens can pursue their individual goals.

Paradoxically, the difficulties of the welfare state cannot be thought to be the result of a lack of achievements. Industrial development and the institutions of the welfare state have in fact reduced human misery. In retrospect, there does not appear to have been any

---

[1]European Communities Statistical Office, *Sozialkonten, 1962–1970* (Luxembourg: 1972); U.S. Bureau of the Census, *Statistical Abstracts of the United States* (Washington, D.C.: U.S. Government Printing Office, 1973, 1974), 1973, p. 286; 1974, p. 273.

alternative strategy compatible with a high degree of political freedom. In the most general terms, the failure of the welfare state rests in its failure to increase its flexibility and to confront its limitations. In this sense, the predicament of the welfare state extends beyond economic formulations. It did not succeed in generating a political, social, and intellectual basis for sustaining and transforming itself. Its accomplishments have not been accompanied by a system of self-generating and self-reinforcing legitimacy. The welfare state is not different from other historical accomplishments.[2] Each epoch brings with it the requirements for social change and adaptation.

However, given the enormous expansion of higher education under the welfare state and the equally extensive allocations of resources for organized "intelligence" and collective problem solving, it had been expected that the welfare state would carry with it, to a greater degree than other epochs, the mechanisms and the capacity for self-redirection and self-generation in institution building. Despite the amount of intellectual effort, this has not been the result, although contemporary dilemmas may well have been deeper and more disruptive without these self-critical standpoints.[3]

Instead, as a result, the essential difficulties of the welfare state have come to rest in its direct effect on the political regime and the resulting inability of the

---

[2]Joseph Schumpeter, *Capitalism, Socialism, and Democracy* (New York: Harper and Bros., 1942); Ralf Dahrendorf, *Class and Class Conflict in Industrial Society* (Stanford, Calif.: Stanford University Press, 1959).

[3]For the alternative point of view see Max Horkheimer, *Eclipse of Reason* (New York: Oxford University Press, 1947).

4

political elites in democratic regimes to govern and effectively modify basic institutions. In each of the parliamentary political systems of the West, the expansion of the welfare system has been accompanied by the emergence of weak political regimes. One of the purposes of this essay is to explore this proposition in some detail. With striking uniformity, the Western parliamentary systems have been unable, during 1965 to 1975, to create governments that command a decisive majority of the electorate. Minority and coalition governments have become a chronic reality. The fragility of the national political consensus can be measured by the instability of the party in power as well as by popular mood and sentiment. The minority and the fragile political regimes are unable to govern effectively. This trend has emerged throughout the Western parliamentary democracies regardless of any differences in their commitments in foreign policy.

No doubt, the changes in social structure and administrative organization are at the root of this process of sociopolitical change. However, it is necessary to assess the extent to which the institutions and practices of the welfare state contribute to political instability. Although there is every reason to assume that the central features of the welfare state will endure and that welfare expenditures will increase, the political mechanisms for administering it will undergo important adaptation if parliamentary regimes are to "master" the stagflation. The problem is whether authoritarian solutions can be avoided—for even a limited increase in authoritarian sanctions would destroy the moral basis and the goals of the welfare state.

Welfare in the Sociological Tradition

Thus, it is necessary to view the difficulties of the welfare state as rooted in economic dimensions—in the new economics—but at the same time to explore these dilemmas as central in the macrosociology of advanced industrial society. In the sociological tradition, there is a core of writings that supply a base for such an agenda. Of course, the classical figures in sociology, from August Comte to Karl Marx to Lester Ward, were concerned with the effect of urbanism and industrialism on the "welfare function."[4] But it was in the 1930s, with the emergence of the new mass programs of welfare, that sociological writings focused on the impact of welfare institutions on social structure. T. H. Marshall, the British sociologist, in *Social Class and Citizenship* traced out the historical process by which citizenship was enlarged and redefined to include the political rights of social welfare.[5] In *Man and Society in an Age of Reconstruction,* Karl Mannheim, the exiled German sociologist, used the awkward phrase "fundamental democratization" to analyze the instabilities of parliamentary rule involved in the expansion of the electorate.[6]

In the post-World War II period, Richard Titmuss in Great Britain and Harold Wilensky in the United

---

[4]Henry Steele Commanger, ed., *Lester Ward and the Welfare State* (Indianapolis, Ind.: Bobbs-Merrill, 1967).

[5]T. H. Marshall, *Citizenship and Social Class* (Cambridge: University of Cambridge Press, 1950); Edward A. Shils. "The Theory of the Mass Society," *Diogenes,* No. 39 (1962): 45–66.

[6]Karl Mannheim, *Man and Society in an Age of Reconstruction* (London: Kegan Paul, 1940).

States have been the chief figures pursuing the analysis of the effect of social welfare institutions on social structure.[7] The basic argument has been offered—and there is every reason to accept it, but only as a point of departure—that the size of national welfare expenditures is a direct function of the size of the per capita gross national product, the length of time that the welfare system has existed, and the size of the old-age population.[8] The thrust of this argument is that among industrialized nations, the form of government and the content of political ideology is not an overriding factor in the amount of welfare expenditures. However, our problem goes beyond such statistical analysis into the consequences and limitations of the welfare state.

Sociologists have therefore been concerned with the extent to which welfare services, plus educational expenditures, have redistributed income. They have assumed that an effective system of social welfare would increase social equality and thereby strengthen the mechanisms of a political democracy. However, increased social welfare payments and more extensive social service expenditures have not been accompanied by a drastic or even marked redistribution of income. It has become inescapable that an important aspect of this issue is the incidence of taxation as well as the resulting incidence of welfare payments.

---

[7]Richard Titmuss, *Essays on "The Welfare State"* (London: Allen and Unwin, 1958); Harold L. Wilensky, *The Welfare State and Equality: Structural and Ideological Roots of Public Expenditures* (Berkeley, Calif.: University of California Press, 1975); Harold L. Wilensky and Charles N. Lebeaux, *Industrial Society and Social Welfare* (New York: Russell Sage Foundation, 1965).
[8]Harold Wilensky, *op. cit.*

Social welfare involves both transfer payments of money and the rendering of a variety of services. In recent years, sociologists have been concerned with the quality of welfare services and in turn with the increasing demand for welfare services. The administrative agencies created to administer a variety of welfare programs have not performed up to expectation in the quality and effectiveness of services offered. Contrary to expectation, the increase in the supply of welfare services has not decreased the demand. The demand for welfare, especially for medical services, has grown enormously and has the potential for continued marked growth. It is almost as if the demand for welfare services in an advanced industrial society is self-generated.

As a result, the issues of social welfare have emerged as a central theme of political debate and protest. In the 1960s, the drama of student protest against the war in Vietnam and against conscription produced a visible state of explosive tension. The deescalation of the United States involvement in Vietnam defused that focal point of conflict; but the underlying tensions associated with the problems of the welfare state constitute the central points of political conflict, even though these have been less likely to erupt in symbolic expressions of protest and/or violence.

In the perspective of sociological analysis, the amount, content, and quality of social welfare services, as much as the level of industrial and economic production, are the central issues of the social order under advanced industrialism. Social welfare has served as a crucial dimension in posing for "modern" sociologists the classic problem, How is it possible for men and women with competing interests and goals to create a social order? The advent of the welfare state only serves to redefine the content and substance of the sociological tradition.

In essence, the dilemmas of the welfare state are expressions of the strains and limitations on the system of social control. "Social control" refers to the ability of a social group or a society to engage in self-regulation.[9] The obverse of social control is coercive control. The macrosociology of an advanced industrial society raises the question of how to organize and manage a system of social welfare without a resort to, or with a minimum of, coercive control. In the intellectual tradition of sociology, social control transformed sociological inquiry at the turn of the century from a speculative enterprise to an empirical research effort.[10] The notion of social control carried with it philosophical implications—concern with higher moral principles—the basis on which social control would be created and the ethical principles and goals to which social groups would aspire. Suddenly, in the 1930s, under the impact of the Great Depression, sociologists departed from these formulations of social control as they became fascinated and preoccupied with issues of power. The result was not an effective sociological perspective for analyzing the complexities of the social

[9]Robert E. Park and Ernest W. Burgess, *Introduction to the Science of Sociology* (Chicago: University of Chicago Press, 1921), p. 766. See also Ralph H. Turner, *On Social Control and Collective Behavior* (Chicago: University of Chicago Press, 1967).

[10]Morris Janowitz, "Social Control and Macrosociology," *American Journal of Sociology*, LXXXI (July 1975), 82–109.

structure and its relation to political power. Instead there emerged an emphasis on oversimplified "power" theories often grounded in gross economic determinist arguments. The idea of social control was temporarily transformed into a pejorative term which came to mean conformity and social repression. But the contemporary problems of the welfare state focus attention on the underlying character of the social order and the issues of social control. Sociologists have been forced to focus increasingly on the total social order of modern society; the conception of social control supplies an indispensable perspective for linking economic processes to the difficulties of welfare institutions. Throughout this essay, the term "social control" will be used in its "classical" and enduring sense, although this is not the fashion in which it is used by many writers.

Welfare and Economic Growth

In essence, the welfare state rests on the availability of some form of economic surplus, or economic profit— individual or social—that can be reallocated in terms of a set of principles. (The issue of mutual self-help, including community self-help, is also crucial and is not overlooked in this formulation.)[11] An economic

---

[11]Mutual self-help implies the availability of some economic surplus either in the form of manpower or economic resources, which is administered on a localistic basis without reference to marketplace considerations but is utilized on the basis of commercial norms. There is often a multiplier element in that self-help makes use of external resources or is able to be effective because it can mobilize economic resources. The notion of self-help has particularly important consequences in welfare because of its symbolic content.

surplus is calculated according to some notion of profit. Of course, the components of profit and the system of calculating economic transitions are arbitrary. But having pointed this out, we must recognize that the conception of profit remains indispensable for analyzing the systems of regulation and self-regulation of the welfare system. The sociologist cannot proceed without a notion of profit, however it is defined. The welfare state rests on the idea that industrial enterprise creates a profit—an economic surplus—that supplies the material basis of the welfare function.

In the contemporary setting, we speak of a system of national accounts rather than profit. National accounts is the total sum of the economic transactions in both private and public sectors. The new terminology does not obscure the observation that the system of national accounts requires some conception of profit that is compatible with the various traditions of economic thinking. In fact, it makes little difference whether one draws on classic economic formulations or on those specifically offered by Marx. The dilemmas of the welfare state can be and must be analyzed in the terminology of profit and the resulting economic surplus. One can speak either in terms of the labor theory of value or of the exchange theory of value. Industrial and commercial enterprises generate profit and an economic surplus, which can be used for social welfare purposes. In the case of Marx, the allocation of this economic surplus is central to his perspective, since it reflects the social relations of society and influences the patterns of social conflict. In simplest terms, "capitalist" societies produce surplus profit that cannot be utilized effectively for the workers' welfare. Instead, surplus profit produces disruption because of the economic business cycle and the pressure for imperialist expansion and imperialist war—both of which create the conditions for political conflict and the transformation of capitalism to socialism and socialism into communism.

However, the structure of the national economy—that is, the pattern of national accounts—for advanced industrial societies under parliamentary regimes has been modified by the welfare state. During the period from 1945 to 1965, these nations were able to produce high rates of economic development and to limit fluctuation in industrial and employment levels as described below. Since 1945 and particularly since 1965, the significance of military expenditure to maintain economic growth and full employment has declined and can hardly be considered basic for the vitality of the economy. To the contrary, the burden of military expenditures has led to limited economic growth. This is not to underemphasize the impact of military establishment on domestic and international affairs.

Below, the available estimates of the relation between military spending and welfare spending, as well as the problematic issue of the impact of capital investments, economic growth, and welfare expenditures are discussed. At this point, it is necessary to point to the pattern, magnitude, and scope of growth in welfare expenditures. The data for selected years from 1929 to 1974 are presented in Table 1. Total expenditures in constant 1974 prices rose from over $10.9 billion to $241.7 billion from 1929 to 1974. In per capita terms, the growth was from $88 in 1929 to $1,125 in

TABLE 1
Growth in Welfare Expenditures in the United States, 1929–1974

Total and per capita social welfare expenditures under public programs in the United States in actual and 1974 prices

FISCAL YEAR	PER CAPITA SOCIAL WELFARE EXPENDITURES IN CURRENT PRICES*								CONSTANT FISCAL YEAR 1974 PRICES		
	TOTAL†	SOCIAL INSURANCE	PUBLIC AID	HEALTH AND MEDICAL PROGRAMS	VETERANS' PROGRAMS	EDUCATION	OTHER SOCIAL WELFARE	ALL HEALTH AND MEDICAL CARE‡	TOTAL SOCIAL WELFARE EXPENDITURES AMOUNT (IN MILLIONS)	PER CAPITA	IMPLICIT PRICE DEFLATORS (1974=100)
1929	$ 31.80	$ 2.78	$ 0.49	$ 2.85	$ 5.31	$ 19.75	$ 0.62	$ 3.87	$ 10,882.4	$ 88.83	36.0
1950	152.56	32.19	16.26	13.34	44.18	43.47	2.92	19.97	44,107.0	287.31	53.1
1955	194.66	58.71	17.98	18.58	28.46	66.68	3.71	26.47	53,916.7	322.82	60.3
1960	285.42	105.35	22.46	24.45	29.52	96.43	6.24	35.03	78,237.6	428.56	66.6
1965	391.15	142.29	31.95	31.76	30.31	142.73	10.50	48.48	109,118.6	554.82	70.5
1970	701.78	262.47	79.48	47.01	42.99	245.23	21.24	121.65	176,472.6	850.64	82.5
1971	818.61	315.28	101.47	52.09	49.08	271.62	24.07	136.51	199,453.2	951.87	86.0
1972	906.72	351.88	123.25	58.71	53.59	286.14	26.86	156.07	216,044.3	1,021.08	88.8
1973	1,001.65	401.83	134.58	59.28	60.13	305.91	29.71	167.98	232,410.9	1,089.93	91.9
1974	1,125.59	456.41	156.58	65.44	64.19	838.66	32.29	192.35	241,736.9	1,125.59	100.0

*Excludes expenditures within foreign countries for education, veterans' payments, and OASDHI and civil service retirement benefits.

†Includes housing, not shown separately.

‡Combines health and medical programs with medical services provided in connection with social insurance, public aid, veterans' payments, vocational rehabilitation, and antipoverty programs.

SOURCE: Per capita figures based on January 1 data from the Bureau of the Census for total United States population, including armed forces and federal civilian employees and their dependents overseas, and the civilian population of territories and possessions. Deflators based on implicit price deflators for personal consumption expenditures prepared for the national income accounts by the Bureau of Economic Analysis, Department of Commerce.

From *Social Security Bulletin* (Washington, D.C.: U.S. Government Printing Office, January 1975), p. 10.

1974, with the level of expenditures more than doubling in the decade since 1965.

The underlying assumption of this analysis is that progressively the relative availability of economic resources with which to underwrite the development and maintenance of the welfare state has declined. In fact, the trend has been toward creating a "negative" surplus in Western industrialized societies.

It needs to be emphasized that obviously we are dealing with the summation of the economic transactions of the private and the public sectors. To speak of a decline of economic surplus is to indicate that the national society (as measured by its national accounts) has come to consume relatively more than it produces. (In this formula the requirements of reinvestment for capital goods are taken into consideration and are crucial.) It is necessary, as will be done below, first to examine the patterns of public accounts and then to proceed to the private sector. The pattern of spending since 1945 indicates the emergence of a chronic deficit in spending by federal as well as by state and local government. But the resources available for welfare—relative and absolute—rest on the articulation of the public sector accounts with those of the private sector.

The economic transactions of the private operate to generate economic resources required to pay economic costs (wages, materials, interests) and to produce profit. A portion of the profit is allocated for reinvestment in capital goods and part is available for transfer by taxes to the system of public accounts. To speak of a decline of economic surplus reflects both the long-term, relative decline in rates of profit and the level of private investment; these indicators again imply the relative decline of available economic surplus.

The negative surplus is described below in terms of the language and categories of national accounts. The emergence of a negative surplus or a chronic economic deficit in the public sector has been a long-term trend. It reflects the system of internal management of investment, profits, and wage allocations. But it also reflects the increased rates of increased social welfare expenditures. The welfare state has become a permanent, or rather a chronic deficit, economy in the public sector accounts. Therefore, the system of social control comes under fundamental strain. The essential dilemmas of the welfare state are those of ineffective social control or self-regulation. The resulting internal political conflict derives in part from the decline of an effective surplus for social welfare and the profound escalation of demand for social welfare.

The difficulties of the welfare state cannot be resolved by increases in the supply alone; a restructuring of the demand for social welfare is required. But at this point there is no need to be limited by economic language. The issue is the potential for institution building to refashion human needs. The content and the definition of the "good society" and the moral order are directly involved. Thus it is intriguing to explore, as a first step, the crisis of the welfare state by beginning with an examination of its intellectual and conceptual origins. It is a dangerous enterprise, since it can lead to an exaggeration of the influence of ideas and of the importance of men with knowledge. But this can be corrected by the second step, namely, an examination of alternative views of the institutional basis from which the welfare state has developed. Both these steps are precursors to the central subject of this paper, that is, the impact of the welfare state on the socioeconomic structure, the political institutions, and the psychological well-being of contemporary society. It is hoped that these observations will supply a stimulus for clarifying the conceptual issues involved in the reconstruction of the welfare state through new forms of institution building—a topic that is explored as the conclusion.

Intellectual Origins
of the Welfare State

II:
The definition of the welfare state includes political control by a parliamentary democracy with an effective legislative opposition.[1] This is not to deny or neglect the welfare functions in a single-party state but to emphasize those democratic political arrangements that have come to be valued along with welfare institutions. Therefore, the history of the idea of the welfare state is part of the history of Western political theory. The component elements of this body of thought and the other essential conceptual elements can be schematized in four categories for the purposes at hand.

First, there is the liberal concept of the modern nation-state. In alternative language, it could be called the secular theory of the modern Western state. There has been an enormous body of literature about "modernization," the result of which makes possible a formulation of the underlying political theory of the Western nation-state. Basically, the Western nation-state arose from the joint processes of urbanization

---

[1]Maurice Duverger, *Political Parties: Their Organization and Activity in the Modern State* (New York: J. Wiley, 1959); Robert Dahl, *A Preface to Democratic Theory* (Chicago: University of Chicago Press, 1956). See also Otto Kirchheimer, "The Waning of Opposition in Parliamentary Regimes," *Social Research*, XXIV (Summer 1957): 117–156.

and industrialization and the concommitant processes of "rationality," as formulated by Max Weber.[2] However, these processes, without the special elements of Westernization, could not account for the particular political sequence that has led to the emergence of the Western nation-state. In other words, there are alternative paths toward modernization.

The emergence of the nation-state in Western Europe and the United States rested on the experiences of 1,000 years of gradual differentiation between religious institutions and the state. The form and content of religion in the West, which facilitated the separation of church and state, contributed to this transformation. This differentiation created the conditions for developing the scientific and technological institutions required by industrialization as well as war making. However, the burden of the argument about the Western experience in modernization rests on the assertion that the separation of church and state created the conditions for the emergence of a secular state. In particular, it produced a state that in varying degrees was compatible with and conducive to an ideology and to institutional building, which in turn resulted in increasing popular participation. The history of Great Britain is taken as the crucial example, especially in comparison with the more discontinuous process of emergence of popular participation in France. But

---

[2]Max Weber, *The Theory of Social and Economic Organization,* trans. A. M. Henderson and Talcott Parsons, ed., Talcott Parsons (New York: Oxford Press, 1964), pp. 329–341. See also E. A. Wrigley, "The Process of Modernization and the Industrial Revolution in England," *Journal of Interdisciplinary History,* III (Autumn 1922): 225–259.

clearly the secularization of the state is not a sufficient conceptual ground or precondition for the emergence of the welfare state.

Elements of Political Philosphy

Second, the welfare state rests on the outgrowth and impact of those political philosophies that justified popular participation in the governmental process and that sought to develop a rationale for parliamentary regimes. The nationalism of the secular Western nation-state required a political philosophy supporting popular sovereignty. Religious motifs of Protestant thought are an important element. But in the history of ideas, the philosophy of John Locke can be taken as representative of the range of political symbolism that justified a parliamentary political regime.[3]

However, the political philosophy on which the welfare state rests includes utilitarianism. Utilitarianism supplied a philosophy and a rationale for applying the apparatus of the state on behalf of the welfare of persons as individuals. There can be no doubt that the utilitarians launched their political critiques to undo what they believed to be the restraining collectivism inherent in the remaining residues of feudalism. But the influence of utilitarianism was to engender a secular basis for collective action by which to create the welfare state. In addition, the utilitarians emphasized

---

[3]George H. Sabine, *A History of Political Theory* (New York: H. Holt, 1937).

the notion of legislation as the mechanism for social reform. As a result, the legislative theories of James Mill, Jeremy Bentham, and John Stuart Mill had the unanticipated consequences of supplying a reasoned basis for constructing social welfare institutions. A. V. Dicey, in his *Lectures on the Relation between Law and Public Opinion in England during the Nineteenth Century,* traced the passage of laws designed to free economic life from archaic, feudal restraints.[4] Such laws could serve as precedents for legislation that would transform charity into the origins of a national system of social welfare. Formulating a system of legislative rules by which the state would be the mechanism for individual and corporate economic development led, step by step, to the idea that the agencies of the state should operate to protect and assist those who were unable to benefit from the expanding industrial processes of the nineteenth century.

Third, if the political philosophy of parliamentarianism, supported by the logic of utilitarianism, justified the emergence of piecemeal welfare legislation, it was the influence of socialism—both religious and economic—that supplied the ideologies that were a driving force for the welfare state. One should not underemphasize the extent to which the elements of religious socialism offered an ethical basis, enabling the welfare system to be compatible with parliamentary institutions.

The various patterns of socialistic thought, as they

---

[4]A. V. Dicey, *Lectures on the Relation between Law and Public Opinion in England during the Nineteenth Century* (London: Macmillan, 1930).

emerged by the end of the nineteenth century, served to reinforce the collectivist basis of state intervention for social welfare.[5] Socialist thought was so powerful and pervasive that it is impossible to think of modern welfare institutions in the absence of these bodies of doctrine. Socialist thought about the welfare state originated partly in religious sentiment. Religious aspirations for communal existence go far back in Christianity. However, the offshoots of the Protestant Reformation contributed to pragmatic socialism, especially in Great Britain.

It would be in error to conclude that the framework of economic socialism of the Marxist or of the social democratic persuasion came to supplant the religious impulse in the drive for the welfare state. Rather, these ideologies supplied a rationalistic critique of industrialism and marketplace economics. Either by revolution or gradually, capitalist society was to be fundamentally transformed, not only by the changes in the ownership of the means of production but also by the construction of new institutions for the formation of human character. No doubt the powerful drift toward secularism and the diffusion of rationalism under industrialism attenuated the explicit role of religious sentiment. But the economic-determinist elements of socialism produced and sustained powerful fractional struggles about the "correct road to socialism." Organized religion, especially of the social gospel variety, supplied an integrative ethical component to

---

[5]Alexander Gray, *The Socialist Tradition: Moses to Lenin* (New York: Longmans Green, 1946).

socialist aspirations. It also supplied a persistent series of agitational leaders who effectively pressed the claims of the welfare state.

No doubt, in the basically secular setting of contemporary United States, religious and altruistic elements are operative, although they are second-order dimensions. In fact, religious definitions of welfare have not been rooted in strong altruism, that is, in powerful sentiments of personal sacrifice—the demonstration of material self-restraint, extensive tithing, or commitments to periodic redistribution of wealth. Rather the religious sentiments have often been expressed by an activist perspective of self-improvement and assistance in the improvement of others, plus the notion of charity. The idea of charity carries with it, in opposition to altruism, the notion of the lesser moral worth of the recipient. There is every reason to believe that this definition of charity continues to be operative in the contemporary system of welfare, especially in family-assistance plans.

But the socialist aspect of the welfare state is complicated. To speak of the religious and economic basis of socialism is to focus mainly on the universalistic dimensions of the welfare state. However, the socialist element of welfare has been easily adapted to nationalism and perverted by ultranationalist aspirations. It was under Bismarck—in the name of German nationalism—that social welfare legislation demonstrated one of its strongest impulses. And let there be no misunderstanding—the phrase "Nazi" stands for "National Socialist German Workers Party," and the socialist impulse under Adolf Hitler kept the social services intact and pressed for the expansion of welfare activities.[6] In the post-World War II reconstruction of Germany, the continuity of these welfare institutions was taken for granted and permitted the society to concentrate on industrial reconstruction.

Impact of Social Science

Fourth, the intellectual and conceptual foundations of the welfare state rest on the traditions of the Enlightenment and the long-term emergence of social science and social research. In this regard, we are dealing not only with broad-scale intellectual movements that contributed to ideological and political aspirations but, as time went on, also with detailed and elaborated bodies of thought and research, which have assisted in the management of social welfare institutions (for better or worse)—that is, with contributions to professional and administrative perspectives.

The Enlightenment involved not only the intellectual events in France but also the Western European emphasis on scientific rationalism. The Enlightenment signified that men are committed to the possibility of an empirical understanding and a codification of human experience and of the real world—physical, biological, and social.[7] The accumulation of knowledge is not only possible; it is also desirable and essential for the betterment of human existence. In a more

[6]Franz Neumann, *Behemoth, the Structure and Practice of National Socialism 1933–1944* (New York: Octagon Books, 1963).
[7]Keith Baker, *Condorcet* (Chicago: University of Chicago Press, 1975).

fundamental sense, there is reason to believe in the long-term potentialities of human betterment. The accumulation of knowledge is in effect an indicator of a belief in the potential of human progress and betterment.

In essence, scientific rationalism is a radical view of mankind—the perfectability of man through knowledge. It is not considered radical because it rests on a belief in the desirability of using violence to seize the instruments of state. The word "radical" has its alternative meaning in the conception of the potentialities of knowledge and human development toward the attainment of rational self-control.

It is a long and tortured path from the spirit of the Enlightenment to the institutional development of social research. But an important stimulus for social science and for the persistent optimism about the consequences of social research is rooted in the continued spirit of the Enlightenment. It is indeed striking that the rise of totalitarianism, with the Russian Revolution and with the seizure of power by the Nazis, did not break this stream of intellectual optimism. Even the destruction during World War II and the extermination of minority groups left these intellectual aspirations relatively intact. In fact, the intellectual community of the Western world after World War II emerged with a powerful commitment to the pursuit of social science knowledge, with the conviction that its accumulation would continue to contribute to human betterment, social welfare, and more effective processes of social control.

The emergence of nuclear weapons shook the optimism of the academic community to a considerable extent. In the United States, it was not until the eruption of student unrest in the 1960s that the unbroken commitment to the optimism of the Enlightenment was extensively called into question. Perhaps these campus events were of coincidental importance. However, it could be that the growing difficulties of the welfare state raised these doubts. The energetic pursuit of social research, which for over a century supplied an important intellectual component in the search for a system of effective social welfare, was directly attacked. One cannot overlook the fact that with the disruption of campus life—of the daily routines of the scholar—the long-standing intellectual optimism was deeply shaken.

In the sociological frame of reference, the empirical data and documentation of poverty and social disorganization have been important intellectually, even more than the conceptual frameworks that sociologists have formulated. The welfare state carried with it a generalized commitment to deal with the findings of the social survey—the efforts to document the realities of nineteenth-century industrialism. The social survey is epitomized by the monumental works of Mayhew and Booth in England, which supplied the factual context for the efforts to eliminate poverty and misery.[8] These efforts were institutionalized in the research of the Fabian Society and of the London School of Economics.

The counterparts in the United States were highly

[8]Philip Abrams, ed., *The Origins of British Sociology, 1834–1914* (Chicago: University of Chicago Press, 1968).

decentralized community surveys sponsored by the Russell Sage Foundation, which were undertakings in local self-development and social planning. The intellectual and analytic core was supplied by "the Chicago school" of empirical sociology, with its close but complicated linkages with the settlement house and the social work movements.[9] In the United States, the social survey became refined and elaborated into the quantitative study of social change. Under the guidance of William F. Ogburn, a body of social statistics was collected and analyzed as the basis for developing effective legislation. The publication in 1933 of *Recent Social Trends in the United States,* the report of President Herbert Hoover's special commission, represented the emergence of the sociological perspective as a national resource for designing the welfare state[10] The contemporary emphasis on social indicators is but a continuation of this long-term focus on the underlying trends of social change.

Sociologists have traditionally been aware of the "intractable" nature of social institutions and the bureaucratic impediments to effective social control. But their writings on these subjects have not profoundly influenced the forms and structure of the welfare state. The writings of the Chicago School on the local community prepared in the 1920s and 1930s dealt with the difficulties and limitations of professional social work and stressed the need for local community

[9]Morris Janowitz, ed., *W. I. Thomas, On Social Organization and Social Personality* (Chicago: University of Chicago Press, 1966). See also Robert E. L. Faris, *Chicago Sociology: 1920–1932* (Chicago: University of Chicago Press, 1970).

[10]*Recent Social Trends in the United States,* vols. I, II (New York: McGraw-Hill, 1933).

organization and citizen participation as devices for controlling bureaucratic trends.[11] Only in the 1960s did the issues of "welfare bureaucracy" come into the focus of attention. With the support of the War on Poverty, there were numerous and widespread experiments in new forms of citizen participation in welfare activities, but they were often launched without sufficient preparation and at times had unrealistic goals.

Psychology, including theories of personality, played a different but central intellectual role in the institutional building of the welfare state. While the results have hardly been adequate for the goals and while there have been grossly distorted consequences, psychology's contributions have been essential. Psychology in part reinforced the ideal of the perfectability of man—the modern version of the Enlightenment—and accordingly assisted in the drive for a rational approach to the goals of the welfare state.

At the core of the contributions of psychology to the welfare state rest the twin approaches of pragmatism—the American formulation—and psychoanalytical psychology—the European accomplishment.[12] At first glance, one would have thought that

[11]Solomon Kobrin, "The Chicago Area Project—a 25 Year Assessment," *Annuals of the American Academy of Political and Social Science,* CCCXXII (March, 1959): 19–29; Irving A. Spergel, ed., *Community Organization: Studies in Constraint* (Beverly Hills, Calif.: Sage Publication, 1972); Peter Marris and Marlin Rein, *Dilemmas of Social Reform: Poverty and Community Action in the United States* (New York: Atherton Press, 1967); Daniel P. Moynihan, *Maximum Feasible Misunderstanding: Community Action in the War on Poverty* (New York: The Free Press, 1969).

[12]See especially John Dewey, *The Public and Its Problems* (New York: H. Holt, 1927); Sigmund Freud, *Introductory Lectures on Psychoanalysis* (London: Allen and Unwin, 1922); *Psychopathology of Everyday Life* (New York: Macmillan, 1914).

psychoanalysis, which emphasizes the biological roots of human behavior and the early formation of personality, could have stood as an intellectual barrier to the welfare state. But, in effect, like pragmatic psychology, its therapeutic methodology points to the possibilities for improving human personality. Both systems of thought served as a rationale for the psychological change required to accomplish the goals of the welfare state. Personality change requires an indulgent environment—a set of goals compatible with those of the welfare state. Both psychoanalysis and pragmatism also emphasize the importance of individual and collective problem solving and of strengthening patterns of personal and social control as opposed to the prospects of conformity and coercion.

It would be a grave error to conclude that with the development of the welfare state there has been a "triumph of the therapeutic," as some commentators claim. That phrase asserts that, in the United States especially, the aspirations of psychology have become the basis of social relations, a standard of performance both for professional social welfare services and for personal self-development. Psychological strategies have at points served to justify or at least rationalize manipulative therapy. Nevertheless, pragmatism and psychoanalytical psychology have no doubt had a direct but difficult to delimit effect on strengthening standards by which the recipients of welfare and institutional treatment should be handled with an element of human dignity. The positive effect of these conceptual processes emerges again and again as an element in a secular definition of morality.

While sociological and psychological analysis stimulated and reinforced the sociopolitical trends toward a welfare state, economic analysis supplied the basis for the essential regulative mechanisms. The model of macroeconomics constructed by John Maynard Keynes was drawn from the mainstream and basic postulates of conventional economics.[13] He offered an economic strategy for dealing with the instabilities and fluctuations of the business cycle. Keynesian economics was a device for creating and redistributing economic resources that made public financing of the expanding institutions of the welfare state possible. This fiscalist strategy for the management of the economy—in a period when socialist perspectives were being fragmented—operated as a comprehensive and integrative ideology for managing the economy.

Keynesian economics supplied an overview of the total society and a detailed procedure for assessing and constructing national accounts. It constructed an image of reality that led directly to political action and legislation. It was a powerful contribution to the mechanisms of social control and the management of the welfare state. For roughly a quarter of a century after 1945, Keynesian economics was the driving force of the political economy of the welfare state. Its basic thrust was that by regulating the governmental budget political leaders had a mechanism for directing the entire economy. It came to represent one of the most conspicuous examples of a direct and lasting influence of intellectual analysis on public policy. Its categories

[13]For an overview of the relevance and limitation of Keynesian economics for public policy see Harry Johnson *On Economics and Society* (Chicago: University of Chicago Press, 1975).

supplied a device for the technical analysis of the economy and a basis for popular political discourse. In essence, it linked the economist, the political leader, and the advocate of social welfare.

No doubt Marxian categories of class structure and class conflict have operated as devices that are even more powerful and effective for political action. Although they are limited in their ability to describe and account for sociopolitical change, these symbols of social class have supplied the basis for organizing powerful political movements that have been able to seize political power and transform national regimes. The vocabulary is particularly attractive to intellectuals, since it has supplied an effective device for their entrance into agitational politics. In this regard, the categories of social class are used as a resource for political agitation and not for analysis. By contrast, Keynesian economics sought and did undergo some significant intellectual development. However, it failed to anticipate and to deal with the changes in social structure that by the middle of the 1960s had created a chronic deficit in governmental accounts and had rendered less and less relevant its particular policy solutions. In the absence of social and political adaptation, Keynesian economics contributes to the emergence of chronic inflation on the one hand and to a decline in concern with increased productivity on the other hand.

The Institutional Base
of the Welfare State

III:

The interplay of the various conceptual strands that helped fashion the welfare state can be considered as producing a slow and gradual process of evolution. In time, the weight of the accumulated results produced the modern system of the welfare state, with its complex programs, its extensive professionalization, and its profound political conflicts. However, there is reason to offer another institutional history of the welfare state, a different overview of the pattern and tempo of its emergence. The pattern of gradual evolution reflects the origins and initial phases. However, there were threshold periods—relatively brief and intense—in which both societal transformations and institution building rapidly created the essential expansion and consolidation of the welfare state. It was as if there had been a long period of maturation and tentative experimentation, and then, from a historical point of view, a threshold was reached in the emergence of the welfare state. The impact of the Great Depression has been cited as the crucial historical event in the development of social welfare in the United States. During the Great Depression, basic categorical programs of income maintenance were established. Paradoxically, students of the history of the welfare state view the events of World War II as also being crucial and as producing another historical threshold on which the welfare state as a comprehensive reality was built.

Great Britain and the United States

There are, of course, very important and persistent differences in the institutional bases of the welfare state in the United States and in Great Britain, but the British experience can be taken as the prototype of welfare institutions under parliamentary governance. No doubt, in part we are dealing with the results of the craft of British social historians who have produced a richer and more interpretative analysis of the expansion of the welfare state than have American specialists.

The welfare state in Great Britain clearly reflects the format of the British governmental structure, with its highly centralized administrative apparatus, its traditional heritage of legitimacy, and its particular forms of resiliency. In contrast to the British governmental development, which emphasizes uniformity and national institutions and standards, the United States federal tradition encourages persistent diversity at the state and municipal levels. Likewise, the scope and form of welfare institutions in Great Britain reflect the influence of a socialist ideology that leads to a stronger emphasis on direct government administration of services, rather than the United States preference for insurance schemes and complex arrangements of indirect payment. Nevertheless, despite the differences in historical background, cultural standards, and tastes, the institutional patterns of development in Great Britain and the United States have important parallels, although the United States lagged behind in level of expenditures and scope of welfare programs.

The British historian of social welfare in the Elizabethan period takes the problem of the "factory child" as one point of departure; for our purposes, it is perhaps sufficient to use the detailed chronology of politics and social policy presented by Derek Fraser in *The Evolution of the British Welfare State*, which highlights the piecemeal steps of the nineteenth and twentieth centuries.[1] One can note that the starting point for the "modern" period may well be the first census of 1801. After that date, in each decade there has been new legislation dealing with health, education, conditions of factory work, and especially payments to the poor.

It would be appropriate to take the results of the Royal Commission on the Poor Law of 1832 and the Poor Law Amendment of 1834, closely linked to the Reform Act of 1832, as a limited and preliminary threshold. The enactment of the Poor Law and the associated political action established the civic obligation of the state to prevent starvation and to ensure subsistence support. The enlargement of private in-

---

[1] Derek Fraser, *The Evolution of the British Welfare State: A History of Social Policy since the Industrial Revolution* (London: Macmillan, 1973). See also Robert Pinker, *Social Theory and Social Policy* (London: Heinemann, 1971).

dustrial enterprise based on competitive norms was in effect joined to a set of collectivist welfare principles and practices. Historians emphasize that the social definition of these benefits under the poor laws contained powerful elements of stigma and disgrace. The emergence of the welfare state required a redefinition of the moral basis of these payments by means of the notions of social insurance, income maintenance, and even negative income tax, but the task is yet to be effectively accomplished. In England, throughout the second half of the nineteenth century, the gradual extension and redefinition of social welfare benefits rested on the expanding political economy of private capitalism. It was, however, with the passage of social and unemployment insurance in 1911 under Lloyd George that a decisive advance was made, an advance that had its impact after World War I.

This heritage of the nineteenth and early twentieth centuries conditioned the social welfare response in Great Britain and the United States to the impact of the Great Depression. Both nations initially sought to impose financial stringency in order to overcome the economics of unemployment. But by 1939, particularly in the United States, the categorical benefits of social welfare were greatly expanded, not only as responses to personal and family needs but also as a strategy of economic expansion.

Perhaps the most significant difference between the institutional bases of the welfare state in Great Britain and in the United States was the emphasis placed on public education—especially for lower-income groups—in the United States. Massive support for the expansion of public education, including higher education, in the United States must be seen as a central component of the American notion of welfare—the idea that through public education both personal betterment and national social and economic development would take place. As early as the 1920s, state universities and municipal colleges had begun their incorporation of lower-middle- and working-class sons and daughters.

No doubt British conceptions of pedigree and social descent were barriers to the expansion of public education, but in part the persistent lower rates of economic growth in Great Britain from the turn of the century implied less economic surplus in the national accounts for the financing of public education. It took the continuous agitation of leaders with a socialist ideology to institute educational reform after 1945.

On the other hand, socialist ideology did not mean that the British welfare state evolved toward an earlier and more extensive implementation of Keynesian management of the business cycle and the expansion of opportunities for employment. The British Labour party has been committed in various degrees to governmental nationalization, but that goal could be implemented politically only on a very segmental basis after 1945. There is no evidence that nationalized industries in Great Britain have outperformed the private sectors, while there is some evidence to the contrary. But the concern with nationalization of industry—as an element in the search for the welfare state—does not account for the reluctance of the Labour party to incorporate Keynesian economics. In part, Keynes himself was not pointed in his policy conclusions until after 1936, although the rudiments of his perspective were clear much earlier. The British Labour party, with its socialist ideology, accepted a traditionalist deflationary budget and monetary policy during the first years of the Great Depression; in fact, Keynes received earlier and wider acceptance in the United States. Thus, Great Britain approached World War II, whose outbreak brought the end of unemployment, with an economic strategy and a set of piecemeal legislative efforts at building social welfare institutions that could only be thought of as a variant on the developments in the United States, despite the important differences between the welfare systems of the two countries.

Impact of World War II

For both nations, the impact of World War II supplied the threshold events that brought the welfare state into being. In Great Britain, World War II had a more visible and a more dramatic consequence symbolically than in the United States. However, the procedures of national wartime mobilization for both countries—and in essence for all of the Western parliamentary democracies—created the essential structure of the welfare state. Writers with diverse assumptions, such as Otto Kirchheimer, R. M. Titmuss, Arthur Marwick, and Derek Fraser, concur in this conclusion.[2]

---

[2]R. M. Titmuss, *Essays on "The Welfare State"* (London: Allen and Unwin, 1958), passim; Arthur Marwick, *Britain in the Century of Total War: War, Peace, and Social Change 1900–1967* (London: Bodley Head, 1968; Boston: Little Brown, 1968). See also Otto Kirchheimer, "Confining Conditions and Revolutionary Breakthroughs," *American Political Science Review*, LIX (December 1965): 964–974.

The welfare state is a political arrangement that emphasizes universalism; mobilization for total war also emphasizes universalism and thus helps create the societal and normative dimensions conducive to the welfare state. The mobilization of World War I was an important step in this direction for Great Britain. But despite the enormous losses and the increasing stress on equality of sacrifice, World War I had only a limited impact on the political thrust toward a welfare state. The consequence of World War I was not the creation of an administrative apparatus capable of implementing the aspirations of the welfare state; this had to await the outcome of World War II, with its organizational developments. Participation in the collective enterprises of World War II—both military and civilian—increased the sense of identity and assertiveness of low-status groups. The events of World War II strengthened the ideal of equality, which continued to grow with profound vigor and impact.

The trends toward the welfare state that evolve during total war are not merely the result of stronger norms of equalitarianism and the stimulation of popular demands for social and economic betterment. In Great Britain, the morale of the home front was sustained not only by Winston Churchill's eloquent propaganda of national survival but also by explicit promises of postwar social reform. These promises were explicitly embodied in the Beveridge Report, prepared under the leadership of William Beveridge, long-time advocate and spokesman for the welfare state. A society that could mobilize for total war was defined as one that could also mobilize for social welfare. Thus it was the actual performance of the central government during the war that was crucial in the thrust toward a welfare state. In essence, the political elites gained the knowledge and the confidence that they could manage the welfare state. The achievements of wartime mobilization created cadres of administrators and administrative structures that could be adapted to large-scale societal innovation. This was in essence a kind of societal "breakthrough," in both the United States and Great Britain. The shift was from limited monetary expenditures for categorical groups to an emphasis on creating new arrangements and new institutions, which were presumed to have the capacity to alter the social structure and assist individuals and their families. Of course, the end of hostilities limited the capacity of the organs of government to intervene, but the threshold of effectiveness that had been achieved was not easily dissipated.

Keynesian economics stood the test of war pressure and was therefore available for financing the welfare state. Social histories of World War II trace the manner in which the economic and welfare schemes that were created during the war supplied the prototypes for the postwar period. Welfare schemes—from mass evacuation of children to extensive food distribution, to new procedures of medical administration, to new community facilities—engendered mass expectations and demands that would not atrophy but required a political response.

When manpower was mobilized for war, the defects of the social order were highlighted in a dramatic fashion. In Great Britain, the Boer War had already revealed the widespread disabilities of the lower classes;

the mobilizations of World War I and World War II made these defects even more inescapable. The United States experienced the same discovery about human resources with similar political discomfort. In both nations, the extensive number of young men who were medically unfit for military service was a startling shock. In Great Britain, the shabby condition of a very large segment of the children being evacuated from the urban centers into the countryside to avoid aerial bombardment left a political stigma. The United States had a similar but less traumatic experience as a result of the extensive wartime migration that brought rural workers, white and black, to the major industrial centers—workers who were almost wholly unprepared for their new life styles.

In Europe, under total war, the distinction between civilians and the military narrowed—a new basis of universalism.[3] In the United States and Great Britain, industrialization and the mobilization of women and minority-group members increased the participation of these individuals in the mass society. It took total war to create both the social and political demands for the welfare state and the social definition of the legitimacy of massive government intervention on behalf of the individual. In Great Britain, the elaborate welfare state as a societal definition came into existence in one dramatic step with the election of the Labour government in 1945. In the United States, while World War II served as the threshold, the societal redefinition was

---

[3]Morris Janowitz, *Sociology and the Military Establishment,* third ed. (Beverly Hills, Calif.: Sage Publications, 1974), pp. 25–42.

not accomplished until the rediscovery of poverty in the 1960s and stimulated by the impact of the civil rights movement. The patterns of social change and social control in the United States reflect the diffuseness of political institutions and the popular ambivalence to the symbols of governmental authority. The institutionalization of the welfare state was in effect delayed until the 1960s, when the problems of its self-regulation were becoming more and more obvious and extensive political onslaught and pervasive intellectual criticisms were becoming operative. It is clear that without massive military mobilization the welfare state would have emerged in Western parliamentary regimes, even if the timing would have been delayed. But the essential historical conclusion remains that it was these events that fashioned the institutional format of the welfare state and supplied the political context.

The Decline
of Economic Surplus

IV:
The theory and practice of the welfare state rest on the ability of the central government to collect and redistribute a portion of the economic surplus of an advanced industrial society. The economy can make use of its economic surplus for the sheer accumulation of wealth, for investment in further capital-goods expansion, for higher private consumption, or for expanded governmental expenditures, including welfare expenditures. The economic surplus that is available for public welfare expenditures rests on the productivity of the economy, an effective tax system, and a system of social and political control that defines the legitimacy of welfare expenditures. The actual expenditures for welfare can be underwritten by current government income or by fiscal borrowing.

At this point it is necessary to examine the assertion that the economic surplus, which the welfare state requires, has been eroding and the governmental budget on which welfare expenditures are underwritten has come to operate with a chronic deficit. This erosion reflects the increased demands for private and governmental consumption in the form of welfare and the reduced ability of the economy to increase productivity and accumulate resources. Because society will not currently pay the full cost of welfare expenditures, the result is a pressure toward inflation and a decrease in the surplus available for capital reinvestment, which in turn contributes to a decline in the growth of economic productivity.

For the sociologist, there is an advantage in thinking of the national economy in terms of the system of national accounts—both in the public and the private sectors—which reflects the totality of economic activity. It is difficult to determine at what point the relative erosion of resources for welfare and the chronic deficit for welfare expenditures arose. It is necessary to examine a variety of economic indicators of the chronic deficit in the government budget and to note long-term limitations in investment and productivity in the private sector. At stake is the supply of economic resources with which to underwrite the welfare state. The erosion of economic resources is a reflection of the system of social control, which has engendered an enormous expansion in the demand for welfare services without an adequate increase in productivity or an effective reduction in private consumption. Subsequently, when examining the effect of the welfare state on social structure and political regime, one must examine the demand for welfare services.

The analysis of the supply and demand for social welfare from a social-control perspective requires an incorporation of economic analysis into macrosociology. Despite widespread efforts to utilize economic constructs for sociological analysis at the level of national accounts and macrosociology, this exploration remains elusive and complex. The major difficulty in applying economic modes of analysis to these sociological problems is not the highly specialized character of economic postulates, namely, those dealing with rational self-interest; the limitations of these postulates are well recognized and can be taken into account. The more pervasive difficulty rests in the arbitrary character of the data on which economic analysis must be based. Each economic transaction generates the operative data for economic analysis and is the result of the existing system of transaction. The procedures of bookkeeping are arbitrary and do not necessarily reflect realities, especially when they involve the welfare system. Economics operate as if the economic transactions adequately reflect the costs involved, and this is not necessarily the case. Likewise, the existing accounting system can markedly distort existing economic "values."

Sociologists have been concerned with the effect of arbitrary and imposed categories on social behavior and their implications for the mechanisms of social control. Sociological literature is replete with analysis of the disruptive impact of the application of psychiatric categories, for example. During World War II, the arbitrary screening of personnel with ineffective testing procedures deprived the armed forces of literally millions of able-bodied men and reduced the nation's capacity to develop its infantry units. The arbitrary nature of the selection system for educational institutions is also very apparent because of social research. However, the system of national accounts and the budgeting procedures of national accounts are taken for granted and unevaluated by sociologists concerned with the welfare state. For example, the fact that there are two systems of budgeting in the United States is generally overlooked. There is one system of accounts for the private sector, which facilitates capital accumulation, since expenditures for capital development are carried as assets. The other system is for the public sector; under it expenditures both for human and for physical capital are carried as liabilities and debts.

By the 1930s, economists had recognized this fundamental defect in the system of national accounts, but there has been no sustained intellectual examination of the influence of existing budgeting procedures on the dilemmas of the welfare state. It might well be the case that a system of accounts that captures public investments as assets in part, and not merely as liabilities, might well have reduced—but hardly eliminated—the contemporary dilemmas of the welfare state. However, the existing categories of economic management are essential ingredients of the process of social control and therefore must be employed as the basis for analysis of the political economy and the welfare state and its dilemmas.

The initial step in obtaining an overview of the transformation of national accounts in the United States is to examine trends in total government spending (all units) as percentages of the national income (Table 2). From these data it can be seen that government spending rose from 11.9 percent of the national income in 1929 to 38.6 percent in 1973. The defense portion of government spending after World War II remained relatively constant, and it has experienced a gradual de-

TABLE 2
Government Spending as a Percentage of
National Income, 1929–1973

YEAR	TOTAL SPENDING	DEFENSE SPENDING	DOMESTIC SPENDING
	a	b	c
1929	11.9	0.8	11.1
1933	26.6	1.5	25.1
1939	24.2	1.6	22.6
1944	56.4	47.9	8.5
1949	27.2	6.1	21.1
1953	33.2	16.0	17.2
1959	32.8	11.5	21.2
1960	32.8	10.8	22.0
1961	34.9	11.2	23.7
1962	34.9	11.3	23.7
1963	34.6	10.5	24.1
1964	33.9	9.7	24.2
1965	33.1	8.9	24.2
1966	34.2	9.8	24.4
1967	37.2	11.1	26.1
1968	38.0	11.0	27.0
1969	37.6	10.2	27.3
1970	37.8	9.3	28.5
1971	37.5	8.3	29.1
1972	39.1	7.9	31.2
1973	38.6	7.0	31.6

a Expenditures of federal, state, and local government as defined in national income accounts.
b Purchases of goods and services for national defense as defined in national income accounts.
c Total spending minus defense spending.

SOURCE: *Economic Report of the President* (Washington, D.C.: U.S. Government Printing Office, 1974), pp. 249, 265, and 328.

cline since 1967. (With the shift from a mobilization military force to a deterrent force in being, military expenditure emerges as much more stable now than in the past.)

The next step is to note the extent to which social welfare expenditures account for a rising fraction of the gross national product and total government expenditures (Table 3). Welfare expenditures as a fraction of the gross national product have risen steadily with the exception of the years during World War II. In 1935, they constituted 9.5 percent of the gross national product; by 1973, the figure stood at 17.6 percent. Welfare expenditures can be measured as a fraction of total government expenditures. On the basis of this measure, there has also been an increase but in a more varied pattern. By 1935, welfare expenditures in the midst of the Great Depression rose to 48.6 percent of total government expenditures. In the post-World War II period of economic prosperity, the figure dropped temporarily to 32.7 percent, but it has been rising steadily, so that in 1973 for federal, state, and local levels it reached 53 percent. It is striking that the upward trend has been even more pronounced at the state and local levels than at the federal level. The patterns of growth of welfare expenditures varied by type of program. On a per capita basis, income maintenance and social security programs expanded approximately 40 times during the period 1935 to 1973; health programs, 23 times; education, 20 times; and veterans' benefits, 12 times.

In partial summary, these data indicate that since 1955 expenditures for social welfare have been less and less the result of a Keynesian policy designed for economic expansion through federal measures. Instead, the logic of social welfare expenditures has become more and more a system of self-sustaining expansion in response to the social and political definitions of welfare requirements.

TABLE 3
Social Welfare Expenditures under Public Programs, 1935–1972
In millions of dollars, except for percentage figures

YEAR	TOTAL SOCIAL WELFARE*	SOCIAL INSURANCE*	PUBLIC AID	HEALTH AND MEDICAL PROGRAMS	VETERANS PROGRAMS	EDUCATION	HOUSING	OTHER SOCIAL WELFARE PROGRAMS	ALL HEALTH AND MEDICAL CARE†	TOTAL SOCIAL WELFARE AS PERCENT OF GNP	TOTAL SOCIAL WELFARE AS PERCENT OF GOVERNMENT EXPENDITURES FOR ALL PURPOSES*
1935	6,548	406	2,998	427	597	2,008	13	99	543	9.5	48.6
1940	8,795	1,272	3,597	616	629	2,561	4	116	782	9.2	49.0
1945	9,205	1,409	1,031	2,354	1,126	3,076	11	198	2,579	4.4	8.4
1950	23,508	4,947	2,496	2,064	6,866	6,674	15	448	3,065	8.9	37.6
1955	32,640	9,835	3,003	3,103	4,834	11,157	89	619	4,421	8.6	32.7
1960	52,293	19,307	4,101	4,464	5,479	17,626	177	1,139	6,395	10.6	38.0
1965	77,175	28,123	6,283	6,246	6,031	28,108	318	2,066	9,535	11.8	42.4
1967	99,710	37,339	8,811	7,628	6,898	35,808	378	2,848	15,823	12.9	42.4
1968	113,840	42,740	11,092	8,459	7,247	40,590	428	3,285	20,039	13.8	43.2
1969	127,741	48,772	13,439	9,004	7,934	44,283	518	3,792	22,934	14.2	44.9
1970	145,894	54,676	16,488	9,753	9,018	50,848	701	4,408	25,232	15.3	47.8
1971	171,901	66,304	21,304	10,800	10,396	56,885	1,047	5,075	28,583	17.0	51.8
1972	192,749	74,715	26,092	12,771	11,465	60,741	1,396	5,569	33,392	17.5	53.4
1973 (prel.)	215,228	85,892	28,327	14,603	12,953	65,247	1,922	6,284	37,554	17.6	55.0

*Although total social welfare and social insurance expenditures include that part of workmen's compensation and temporary disability insurance payments made through private insurance carriers and self-insurers, such private payments have been omitted in computing percentages relating to all government expenditures.
†Combines health and medical programs with medical services provided in connection with social insurance, public aid, veterans and other social welfare programs.

source: *Statistical Abstracts of the United States* (Washington, D.C.: U.S. Government Printing Office, 1973, 1974), 1973, p. 286, and 1974, p. 273.

47

Economic Trends

First, the growth in welfare expenditures needs to be examined in the context of increasing deficit spending both in the public and the private sector. The welfare state has, in effect, been accompanied by an expansion of the propensity to consume more than is produced. A simple and crude approach to measure the chronic economic deficit is to focus on the long-term trends in the federal budget and in particular to note the patterns of deficit spending linked to the rise of the welfare state (Table 4). The major elements in the deficit are the result of military and social welfare expenditures, plus the charges for debt service. The original Keynesian strategy was postulated on a cyclical pattern of government deficit spending to prevent unemployment and contraction of industrial production, followed by a "balanced," or positive, budget designed to prevent excessive inflationary pressures. These trend data clearly reveal that the United States government has entered a pattern of a long-term budget deficit spending. For the period after the Korean War until 1975, during only four years was there a budget surplus, which totaled $10.8 billion, while in 18 years there was a total budget deficit of $182 billion. Moreover, for the fiscal year 1976 a minimum deficit of $68 billion has been constructed.[1]

---

[1]Another indicator of the long-term decline in economic surplus has been manifested in the drop in the United States official reserve assets. A variety of factors and components are involved, but fundamentally this drop reflects the weakened economic position of the United States and the long-term propensity to "consume" at a greater rate than the economy is able to produce. In 1946, the United States official reserve

These data do not encompass the full scope of the governmental budgeting system and the resulting deficits. (*a*) The chronic deficit in the federal budget is increased by financing through intergovernmental exchanges and governmentally sponsored financial agencies that are not fully revealed in the annual federal budget. These transactions increase the long-term federal debt. In addition, for example, the social security system has entered into a deficit state. In 1975 the trustees of the social security fund anticipated a major and growing deficit in available reserves. In order to meet the obligations already incurred, they believed that an increase in the payroll tax from the 1975 level of 11.7 percent by 5.3 percentage points would be required. It is largely a truism to assert that each generation pays in part the claims generated by the previous one; but research analysts can measure the heavy burden contemporary workers have in paying off the social security of the last generation.[2] (*b*) The resources available for welfare and education must be calculated in terms of the negative surplus created by state and local governments and the wide range of special instrumentalities that these governmental units have created. The total outstanding state debt, not including local units, stood at $18.5 billion in 1960 and reached $47.9 billion in 1970; during no year of this period of economic growth and prosperity was there an overall

assets stood at $20.7 billion; in 1971, it reached a low of $12.1 billion; and in 1973, it experienced its first limited increase to $14.3 billion. But the prospect is for pressure on the official reserve assets in the downward direction.

[2] Joseph A. Pechman, *Social Security: Perspective for Reform* (Washington, D.C.: The Brookings Institution, 1968).

TABLE 4
Growth in Federal Deficit Spending,
1929–1976
Federal budget receipts and outlays in millions of dollars

FISCAL YEAR	RECEIPTS	OUTLAYS	SURPLUS OR DEFICIT
1929	3,862	3,127	734
1933	1,997	4,598	−2,602
1939	4,979	8,841	−3,862
1940	6,361	9,456	−3,095
1941	8,621	13,634	−5,013
1942	14,350	35,114	−20,764
1943	23,649	78,533	−54,884
1944	44,276	91,280	−47,004
1945	45,216	92,690	−47,474
1946	39,327	55,183	−15,856
1947	38,394	34,532	3,862
1948	41,774	29,773	12,001
1949	39,437	38,834	603
1950	39,485	42,597	−3,112
1951	51,646	45,546	6,100
1952	66,204	67,721	−1,517
1953	69,574	76,107	−6,533
1954	69,719	70,890	−1,170
1955	65,469	68,509	−3,041
1956	74,547	70,460	4,087
1957	79,990	76,741	3,249
1958	79,636	82,575	−2,939
1959	79,249	92,104	−12,855
1960	92,492	92,223	269
1961	94,389	97,795	−3,406
1962	99,676	106,813	−7,137
1963	106,560	111,311	−4,751
1964	112,662	118,584	−5,922
1965	116,833	118,430	−1,596
1966	130,856	134,652	−3,796
1967	149,552	158,254	−8,702
1968	153,671	178,833	−25,161
1969	187,784	184,548	3,236
1970	193,743	196,588	−2,845
1971	188,392	211,425	−23,033
1972	208,649	231,876	−23,227
1973	232,225	246,526	−14,301
1974	264,932	268,392	−3,460
1975 (estimate)	278,750	313,446	−34,696
1976 (estimate)	297,520	349,372	−68,000

Note: Data for 1929–1939 are according to the administrative budget, and those for 1940–76, according to the unified budget. Certain interfund transactions are excluded from receipts and outlays beginning with 1932. For years prior to 1932 the amounts of such transactions are not significant. Refunds of receipts are excluded from receipts and outlays.

sources: Department of the Treasury and Office of Management and Budget.

positive balance in state financing. In addition to this debt structure, there are a variety of public corporations whose obligations are without full governmental authorization; they are the so-called morally obliged bonds. Of course, it would be interesting if these debt structures—federal, state, and local—included a translation of those portions that created capital resources, but such a translation is impossible given the existing symbols of government and the operating budget procedures of the welfare state.

Second, the political economy of the welfare state can be assessed in terms of the rate of economic growth over the three decades since the end of World War II. It can be argued that an advanced industrial society cannot permanently—that is, over the long run—sustain high rates of economic growth. In other words, the general pattern of growth—the S curve of growth—is applicable, in that high rates of growth must at some point level off. This consideration has some validity, but it was of secondary importance for 1945 to 1975. Comparisons between the major Western industrialized nations are presented below. Overall trends of economic growth can be discerned that are not linked to idealized notions of growth. Or the issue can be stated otherwise: there are specific levels of growth needed for the goals of the welfare state, and it is possible to judge whether these levels have been met, since some Western industrialized nations have achieved them (particularly West Germany) and the United States has not.

For the purposes at hand, the capacity of an advanced industrial society to sustain economic growth adequate for the welfare state can be thought to result (*a*) from economic policies and (*b*) from the social organization of work and industrial enterprise. One set of useful data on long-term economic growth is presented in Table 5. These data can be matched against the arbitrary standard that about 3 percent annual per capita growth is required to produce the economic surplus for the welfare state; probably 3.5 percent is a more reasonable figure if some expansion is sought. This standard includes the goals of greater social equality plus the changes in the population structure, namely the increase in the old-age dependent segments.

It is instructive that in Great Britain a long-term rate of economic growth—about 2 percent—has been operative since World War I and in effect prior to that period. This growth level has never fully satisfied the economic demands of the welfare state. The development of the welfare state in Britain has taken place under conditions of a declining level of income relative to the rest of Western Europe. By contrast, France, Germany, and Italy transformed their economies after World War II and were able to sustain high rates of economic development through the entire period until the emergence of rising unemployment and chronic inflation in the early 1970s.

Since 1945, in the United States the overall rate of economic growth has been somewhat higher than that of Great Britain but below that of Germany, France, and Italy. Because the standard of living is so much higher, it can be argued that a lower rate of economic development is compatible with the requirements of

TABLE 5
Growth Rates of Domestic Produce in Seven Major Industrialized Nations, during Selected Periods, 1913–1971

In percent. Rates are derived from data adjusted for price changes and represent average annual compounded changes in real output from initial to terminal year of period.

PERIOD	UNITED STATES		CANADA		FRANCE		GERMANY*		ITALY		GREAT BRITAIN		JAPAN	
	TOTAL	PER CAPITA	TOTAL	PER CAPITA	TOTAL	PER CAPITA	TOTAL	PER CAPITA	TOTAL	PER CAPITA	TOTAL	PER CAPITA	TOTAL	PER CAPITA
1913–1929	3.1	1.7	2.4	0.7	1.7	1.8	0.4	-0.1	1.8	1.2	0.8	0.3	3.9	(NA)§
1929–1950	2.9	1.8	3.2	1.8	0.0	-0.1	1.9	0.7	1.0	0.3	1.6	1.2	0.6	(NA)
1929–1971	3.2	1.9	3.9	2.1	2.6	2.1	4.2	3.0	3.2	2.5	2.2	1.7	5.1	(NA)
1950–1960	3.2	1.4	3.9	1.2	4.8	3.9	8.5	6.9	5.5†	4.8†	2.8	2.4	8.2‡	7.0‡
1950–1971	3.6	2.1	4.6	2.4	5.3	4.3	6.5	5.2	5.4†	4.6†	2.7	2.3	9.6‡	8.5‡
1960–1971	3.9	2.6	5.2	3.5	5.7	4.6	4.7	3.8	5.2	4.5	2.7	2.1	10.6	9.5
1965–1970	3.3	2.2	4.7	3.1	5.8	5.0	4.7	4.0	5.9	5.3	2.4	2.0	12.1	10.9
1970–1971	2.5	1.5	5.5	4.2	5.1	4.1	2.7	1.7	1.5	0.7	1.6	1.2	6.3	5.0

*Federal Republic of Germany. Beginning 1960, includes Saar and West Berlin.
†Initial year 1951.
‡Initial year 1952.
§NA means not available.
SOURCE: U.S. Bureau of Economic Analysis. Adapted from *Long Term Economic Growth, 1860–1970*, using data from the Organization for Economic Co-operation and Development, as reported in U.S. Bureau of the Census, *Statistical Abstract of the U.S.: 1974* (Washington, D.C.: U.S. Government Printing Office, 1974), p. 374.

the welfare state. However, on a per capita basis, the level of development has been generally below the standard of 3 percent on a decade-by-decade average. Moreover, when one examines the overall trend on an annual basis, the emergence of a declining trend can be seen. Clearly, the long-term trend data on economic growth highlight the difficulties of the political economy of the welfare state in the United States.

Third, stagflation has produced a short-term trend toward chronic inflation, especially if one applies the criterion of more than 5 percent annual increase in the consumer price index (Table 6). For the United States, increases in the consumer price index of more than 5 percent were recorded in 1969 (5.3) and 1970 (5.9). But the impact was decisively registered in 1973, since the percent increase was 6.2, and in 1974, when it reached 11.0 percent. Between the major industrialized nations, there are marked differences in the extent to which the new economics is operative. For example, in 1973 the rate of inflation in Germany was 6.5 per-

TABLE 6
Rates of Inflation in the United States, 1967–1974,
Measured by Percent of Change in
Consumer Price Index
1967 dollars

1974	11.0
1973	6.2
1972	3.3
1971	4.1
1970	5.9
1969	5.3
1968	4.2
1967	2.9

SOURCE: Consumer Price Index, Bureau of Labor Statistics.

cent; in France and Italy it was markedly higher, over 10 percent, and in Great Britain it exceeded 20 percent. These differences—especially in the case of Germany—reflect differing patterns of social control, as discussed below.

The fourth measure related to the relative decline of economic resources for welfare services is the pattern of capital investment. Economists have argued extensively about the level of capital investment required for an advanced industrial society. However, even within the limits of the debate, the United States' economy presents its welfare state with a constricted pattern of capital accumulation in the private sector. The basic comparative data on investment productivity and economic growth are presented in Table 7 for seven major industrialized nations. For the period 1960 to 1973, in the United States national output devoted to so-called fixed investment averaged 17.5 percent. This was lower than in Japan, West Germany, and France, which had high percentages (24 percent or more), and lower even than in Canada, Italy, and Great Britain, which had low investment percentages. This table also presents the rankings of investment percents and output growth percents. The United States is at the bottom of both ranks except that it has a higher output growth percent than Great Britain. The United States is also shown during this period as having the lowest average annual rate of growth for gross domestic product per person and for manufacturing output per manhour.

Fifth, the obverse of capital accumulation for industrial development is the growth of consumer credit.

The expansion of consumer credit represents both current and future economic deficits. It is impossible to redistribute the consumer debt by the mechanism of the welfare state, although steady inflation reduces its impact on some sectors of society. Outstanding consumer credit rose from $21.5 billion in 1950 to $159 billion in March 1973. This rate of growth far exceeded

TABLE 7
Investment and Economic Growth in Seven Major Industrialized Nations, 1960–1973

A. Investment as percent of real national output, 1960–1973*

	TOTAL FIXED†	NONRESIDENTIAL FIXED
United States	17.5	13.6
Japan	35.0	29.0
West Germany	25.8	20.0
France	24.5	18.2
Canada	21.8	17.4
Italy	20.5	14.4
Great Britain	18.5	15.2
11 OECD Countries (1960–1972)	24.7	19.4

*OECD concepts of investment and national product. Data for 1973 estimated.
†Including residential.

B. Investment ratios and growth rates of real output, 1960–1973*

	INVESTMENT RATIO PERCENT	RANK	OUTPUT GROWTH RATE PERCENT	RANK
Japan	29.0	1	10.8	1
West Germany	20.0	2	5.5	3
France	18.2	3	5.9	2
Canada†	17.4	4	5.4	4
Great Britain†	15.2	5	2.9	7
Italy	14.4	6	5.2	5
United States	13.6	7	4.1	6

*Data estimated for 1973.
†Data applied to 1961–1973 are not strictly comparable to data presented for other countries.

C. Productivity growth, 1960–1973 (average annual rate)

	GROSS DOMESTIC PRODUCT PER EMPLOYED PERSON	MANUFACTURING OUTPUT PER MANHOUR
United States	2.1	3.3
Japan	9.2	10.5
West Germany	5.4	5.8
France	5.2	5.8
Canada	2.4	4.3
Italy	5.7	6.4
Great Britain	2.8	4.0
11 OECD Nations	5.2*	6.1

*Average for 6 OECD countries listed.

SOURCE: H. I. Liebling and J. Jackson, "Investment, Productivity and Growth in Major Industrialized Countries," *Review of Economic and Financial Developments* (March 21, 1975).

the growth of the gross national product. Moreover, consumer credit as a ratio of disposable income rose from 10.4 percent in 1950 to 18.07 percent in 1973. In other words, with the advent of stagflation almost 20 percent of disposable personal income in the United States represented consumer credit—the mortgaging of future personal earning. This measure thereby is a pointed indicator of the deficit, which has arisen under existing economic practices of social welfare. In fact, the long-term pattern of deficit spending by the federal government, the increase in state and local obligations, and the measures of limited growth in economic productivity highlight the chronic economic dilemmas of the welfare state.

No doubt, during the two decades after 1955 and even during the last decade, from 1965 to 1975, the United States has had the industrial capacity for a higher rate of economic growth, which could have produced an increased economic surplus for social welfare. Institutional barriers inherent in the organization of industry and the labor force, as much as economic policies, have contributed to the more limited growth of economic productivity. If the crisis of a capitalist society were derived from its inability to dispose of its surplus, the contemporary political economy and the requirements of the welfare state would have eliminated that "problem"—for an economic surplus in the national accounts no longer exists. There have been efforts in the United States to prevent deficit spending by placing aspects of social welfare programs on a "pay as you go" basis. In particular, real take-home wages are decreased to a noteworthy degree by increasing the level of payroll taxes (FICA) for social security. Relevant as such steps have been, they are not of sufficient magnitude to have decisive consequences for the system of national accounts; these steps do not create an effective surplus to underwrite social welfare expenditures.

Alternative Allocations

The assessment of the economic dilemmas of the welfare state must face the double question of whether (a) a drastic reduction in military expenditures and (b) alternative national policies concerning the procurement and use of raw materials and the management of the environment during 1945 to 1975 (as well as for the decades to come) would have and could have decisively altered the resulting economic allocations. In other words, to what extent has the destruction of the Keynesian strategy of economic management been the result of the costs of war—past, present, and anticipated in the future—and to what extent has it reflected misallocations of basic economic resources? Obviously, and unfortunately, no clear-cut answer is possible. However, the available data and the logic of analysis of a social-control perspective point to a more limited conclusion. Alternative economic resource allocation and utilization could well have reduced or mitigated the political difficulties of the welfare state but could hardly have avoided them.

For military expenditures, the hypothetical issue can be stated in terms of the potential consequences for the political economy of a 50 percent reduction in federal expenditures for national defense. Such a reduction is obviously not politically feasible; moreover, such a reduction would most probably lead to the proliferation of independent nuclear weapons systems, especially in Western Europe, and profoundly increased international instabilities and tensions. It is probably true that a 20 percent reduction could be achieved, and I have outlined the basis for such a reduction elsewhere.[3] It must be emphasized that effective reductions in military expenditures can be accomplished only on a step-by-step basis if they are to be real and lasting. Crash programs have strong socially and politically disruptive effects, especially if they violate the contractual agreements that the military has generated in recruiting personnel. Nevertheless, the figure of 50 percent (and also of 20 percent) is designed to explore drastic alternatives. One alternative would be to estimate the consequences had there

---

[3]Morris Janowitz, "Volunteer Armed Forces and Military Purpose," *Foreign Affairs,* L (April 1972): 428–443.

been no direct U.S. military involvement in Vietnam; over the long run, the effect of such a military policy on social welfare expenditures would appear to have been more limited than a 20 percent reduction in annual military expenditures.

Comparisons of the patterns of expenditures on welfare and the military among the major states in Western Europe can be made. There seems to be little relationship between the size of the military budget and the economic resources available for welfare in Western Europe, especially when institutional (age of the welfare system) or demographic (age of population) variables are considered.[4] Moreover, for these nations there is no reason to believe that lower military expenditures during 1965 to 1975 would have increased the effective economic resources available for welfare or reduced the impact of the stagflation. Thus, for example, France has the lowest proportion in military expenditures—about 3 percent of the gross national product—but its rate of inflation has been relatively higher.

The hypothetical analysis of a 50 percent reduction (or a 20 percent reduction) must be examined in terms of the economic logic for the United States per se. Two elements are involved. First, there is the argument that the reduction in military expenditures would produce economic resources that could be directly allocated to the federal welfare budget. Then the amount of resources for welfare would be directly in-

---

[4]Harold Wilensky, *The Welfare State and Equality: Structural and Ideological Roots of Public Expenditures* (Berkeley, Calif.: University of California Press, 1975), pp. 70–85. See also Bruce Russett, *What Price Vigilance? The Burdens of National Defense* (New Haven, Conn.: Yale University Press, 1970).

creased, and the inflation pressures which would thwart the goals of the welfare state would also be reduced in turn. Second, the more sophisticated argument is offered that the pattern of military expenditures since 1945 has resulted in a malfunction in the process of capital formation that greatly hinders economic growth in an advanced industrial society. Some critics hold that contemporary military expenditures alter the research and development function from industrial modernization to military technology with little multiplier, or positive, effect for the national economy.

These arguments need to be examined in the light of the long-term trend in military national defense expenditures since 1945. As indicated above, there has been a long-term decline in the percentage of the gross national product allocated to defense expenditures, which all sources agree upon, although there is disagreement about the magnitudes involved. Moreover, this trend does not rule out short-term fluctuation, especially increases due to strategic weapons procurement. In part, the differences reflect different definitions of the costs of national defense. Official Department of Defense indicators show that there has been a long-term decline each year since 1955, except for a short-term increase during the Vietnam War, from 1967 through 1971. In terms of percentage of the gross national product reported in constant 1958 dollars, the trend was as follows: 1946, 19.4 percent; 1955, 10.2 percent; 1965, 7.5 percent; and 1975, 5.6 percent.[5]

---

[5]Department of Defense, Directorate of Information Operations; Office of the Assistant Secretary of Defense, Comptroller.

Other definitions would include debt services, veterans' benefits, and nonmilitary agency support of defense activities. However, such accounting should include the extensive nonmilitary expenditures of the defense agencies. The rate of decline of military expenditures as a percentage of the gross national product had slowed up by 1975. This was in part due to the fact that the costs of the all-volunteer force are high and will continue to rise, even with a gradual reduction in the force's size.

Thus, a 50 percent reduction in the military budget would produce about a 2.5 percent increase in the gross national product for welfare, while a 20 percent reduction would amount to slightly over 1 percent. Clearly, such resources would contribute to an economic surplus for welfare. Given the increasing demand for social welfare, it is doubtful whether the results would be decisive in modifying the chronic economic deficit in governmental spending. However, a higher economic growth rate would be more decisive in the long run.

It is essential to keep in mind that with the growth of welfare expenditures, military allocations are not required for countercyclical policies. In fact, the positive effect of a reduction of defense expenditure in the United States, as Stanley Lieberson has demonstrated, with the exception of three or four states, would produce a compensatory expansion of civilian goods and services industries. This in turn would yield increased tax revenue, a portion of which would be available for social welfare since the rate of return in nondefense industries is higher than in defense industries.[6] Moreover, it is central to this analysis of the problems of the welfare state that the basic issues rest not merely on the magnitude of the allocations but also on the relevance and effectiveness of the services offered and their consequences for the quality of life. The difficult political issue of making allocations among competing programs is paramount. Again and again, it must be acknowledged that in the absence of effective social control mechanisms to deal with these problems and in the absence of standards to define the limits of welfare services modest increases in the welfare expenditures hardly resolve underlying dilemmas. The essential issue is the overall political control and management of the welfare economy.

The additional argument that focuses on the distortion of capital formation caused by extensive military expenditures, especially in the area of research and development, cannot be dismissed. However, it is difficult to estimate the extent and magnitude involved. In particular, the argument assumes that limitations on economic development in the United States have been technological, either in regard to the level of advanced technology or the extent of modernization of the plant. There is no reason to believe that the most advanced technology is not available for industrial production, although there is some evidence that in certain industries modernization has lagged. No doubt, while the rate of increase of economic productivity is influenced by the technological base and thus by the level of capi-

[6]Stanley Lieberson, "An Empirical Study of Military-Industrial Linkages," *American Journal of Sociology*, LXX (January 1971): 562–584.

tal investment, the forms and practices of industrial organization and management are even more important in accounting for the different rates of economic growth in the United States and, for example, in Germany.

As for resource procurement and utilization, a stronger case could be made that misallocations have contributed extensively to the difficulties of the welfare state. However, the analysis transcends economic dimensions and involves social norms concerning consumption. To what extent are the difficulties of the welfare state under advanced industrialism, as in the United States, linked to uneconomical and in fact irrational allocations of basic resources? It is necessary, of course, to examine a previous question. To what extent has the availability of "cheap" raw materials imported from the developing nations contributed to the past economic base of the welfare state? To what extent have the rising standard of living and the welfare state of the advanced industrialized nations been built on the favorable terms of trade between the European metropole and the United States, on the one hand, and the politically dependent nations whose economies have operated mainly on the production of raw materials, especially for energy, on the other hand.

Undoubtedly, the industrialized nations have benefited from favorable terms of trade in the past. The question is how much, and this appears almost impossible to answer. The dependent nations have received various forms of economic and technical assistance from the industrialized nations, which in time permits certain dependent nations to develop self-sustaining, growth economies. Moreover, the advantages of the cheap raw materials, especially oil, have led to profound distortions in the economies of the advanced nations and to crash efforts to develop more balanced energy programs, which are both costly and disruptive. In any case, the long-term trends have been to eliminate, and even temporarily to reverse, the advantages the advanced industrialized nations had had in terms of trade. Oil is, of course, the crucial case. Moreover, there is little reason to believe that the favorable trade terms in the past have been decisive in determining the patterns of economic growth and in creating resources available for the emergence of the welfare state. Particularly during the decisive period from 1945 to 1975, the economies of the welfare states have been built on technological developments, transformation of industrial organization, and larger and more integrated domestic markets, such as the European Common Market. These factors have their built-in limitations, and even if the costs of raw materials had not risen sharply for the advanced industrialized nations, it is likely that the tensions of stagflation would have emerged. The expanded demand for social welfare and the decline in the available economic surplus for welfare would have become operative after a period of time.

The problem concerning the utilization of resources—including energy resources—related to the internal economy of the advanced industrial nations (and to the economic flows among these nations) rather than to international relations between the industrialized and the developing nations. The main problem of resource utilization within the industrialized nations involves the "classical" issue of the obsolescence—real or contrived—of material goods. This issue can be stated in terms of the fetishism for material objects, as Karl Marx sought to describe it, or in Ralph Nader's popular language, of the waste and useless obsolescence generated for the purposes of increased market consumption. The economic magnitudes are not minor; they can be estimated at from 5 to 20 percent of the total gross national product.

The relevance of material waste and contrived obsolescence for social control of the welfare state does not rest merely in the economic surplus, which would otherwise be available for welfare institutions and expenditures. It involves the basic normative patterns associated with an economy based on high product obsolescence. These issues encompass the social and psychological effects of an advanced industrial society and its welfare institutions and will be explored below. However, there is no need to accept the assertion of writers such as Norman O. Brown or Herbert Marcuse that the underlying discontent of an advanced industrial society is inherent in the restraints on gratification it must impose on its members.[7] This is much too stringent a form of economic and technological determinism. It is more productive to assert, as sociologists have since Emile Durkheim, that the

[7] Norman O. Brown, *Life Against Death: The Psychoanalytical Meaning of History* (Middletown, Conn.: Wesleyan University Press, 1959); Herbert Marcuse, *Eros and Civilization: A Philosophical Inquiry into Freud* (New York: Vintage Books, 1955).

growth of material well-being and economic surplus as a result of industrial production has not necessarily been accompanied by any increase in personal happiness. In good measure, this is because of the absence of a normative definition that could articulate with higher standards of living. In brief, systematic obsolescence and the social definition of consumption stimulated by mass advertising contribute to the inability of increased material well-being to create, for important segments of the population, personal satisfaction and effective indulgence. This is what is meant by "consumerism," the social arrangements under which increased material consumption creates only demands for more indulgence, with resulting personal dissatisfaction.

Consumerism implies that the utilization of material goods does not necessarily relieve deprivation or sublimate frustration but becomes in part an act with aggressive overtones. Material objects and related services are highly esteemed goals and values, but their acquisition and consumption are not without negative consequences, and there is considerable ambivalence toward them. In other words, consumerism is an attitude toward material wealth which helps explain the level of unhappiness and discontent in contemporary society.

This attitude diffuses and sets the context for social welfare and the consumption of social welfare goods and services. Social welfare implies a system of redistribution of goods and services. The social definitions of persons who make use of these goods and services reflect the values and responses of the larger society

As a result, the social psychology of consumerism influences the definitions and responses to social welfare benefits and services and contributes to their inability to satisfy human needs.

The issue is not only the social psychology of consumerism. More concretely, in terms of economic difficulties particular long-term patterns of investment have been dysfunctional. In the United States, investments in transportation supply a crucial example of the negative consequences of resource allocation. In the United States, transportation policy has been built on the development of the automobile and on the private ownership and use of the automobile. Government allocations have been mobilized to permit the maximum expression of the current preference for this mode of transportation. (The use of truck transport represents the effect of organized pressure-group interests. However, the development of truck transportation has facilitated the expansion of the individual automotive system.) Clearly, the automobile offers important short-term advantages and powerful personal gratifications, but its implications for the structure of metropolitan life have been highly disruptive. The social and cultural organizations of the metropolitan centers have been undermined by the unregulated deconcentration of population. The system of automotive transport has contributed to the patterns of residential and personal mobility that have attenuated essential patterns of social cohesion and social solidarity required for personal and civic responsibility. It is not a pointless exercise to speculate about what the United States' economy and the structure of the social order, including its welfare system, would be if the United States had maintained a viable mass transportation system.

Nevertheless, the contemporary economic problems of the welfare state may well be lodged less in the results of past misallocation of resources and more in a political economy that has created a chronic pattern of inflation. "Inflation" here arbitrarily means an increase in the consumer price level that exceeds 5 percent a year. Alternatively, the new economics imply high rates of unemployment (over 6 percent) in the effort to control inflation; such rates are politically and morally difficult to accept as well as socially highly disruptive. There is, of course, no reason to project as inevitable a continuation of the high rate of inflation of the first half of the 1970s. Economists are naturally divided about the scope, causes, and duration, as well as the strategies of solving the "new inflation," which has been accompanied by high levels of unemployment. The differences that separate the economists into the monetarists and the fiscalists are less important for present purposes than the recognition that the inflation, accompanied by a high level of unemployment, implies a transformation in economic structure so extensive that applying the Keynesian strategies would not be sufficient or effective.[8]

As a result, inflation deepens the difficulties of the political economy of the welfare state. First, and obviously, the unemployment associated with the new type

---

[8]Examination of the variety of writings of John Maynard Keynes indicates that he was fully aware and interested in monetary strategies for managing economic growth and controlling inflation.

of inflation requires additional expenditures for welfare and implies a reduction in the funds available for welfare expenditures because of the loss of government tax revenue. In fact, the increased costs under inflation require the federal government to lengthen unemployment compensation. In turn, direct work relief is necessary and becomes a major element of social welfare. Such work relief has been redefined as employment by the government, the employer of last resort, whose goal is creating productive work. However, the economic transactions involved will record these expenditures as costs and liabilities.

Second, inflation clearly means that the resources available for social welfare will decline or be restricted. The government program of budgeting is such that fixed costs and standard programs receive priority on available revenues. Legislative allocations for social welfare thereby produce increased political debate and struggle. Inflation periods are accompanied by a decline in the growth of economic productivity, and thereby the economic surplus for social welfare is further constricted. Paradoxically, there is some countertrend in the available strategies of tax relief. During a period of inflation plus high levels of unemployment, there is pressure for tax relief, which assists the lowest income groups.

Third, while there are particular segments of the social structure that benefit or at least have a vested interest in mild or moderate inflation, the major impact of inflation is negative, in different degrees, on wide segments of society. There is no reason to accept the proposition that inflation—or rather limited inflation—is a device for effective income redistribution. To the contrary, mass opinion has come to be more concerned with the impact of inflation than with that of unemployment. At the height of unemployment in the United States in 1975, public opinion surveys recorded roughly the following public definition of what was the major economic problem; inflation, 70 percent; unemployment, 25 percent; and other, 5 percent. The variation by income group was most limited.

The experiences of Weimar Germany have made the social impact of inflation and its effects on welfare a great concern to sociologists, particularly to political sociologists. Inflation, even inflation of moderate proportions, has come to be seen as undermining the political legitimacy of the parliamentary system. However, there is little by way of empirical research to assess the specific impact on social strata or occupation groupings of the inflationary trends that the United States has experienced since the end of World War II. Moreover, contemporary social structure, because of the rise of the welfare state, is markedly different than that of the interwar years. Thus, it is necessary to examine next the extent to which sociologists have produced pertinent findings about the transformation of social stratification and social structure under the growth of the welfare state. The trends are relevant for understanding social control in the light of the new economy and the declining economic surplus for social welfare.

Trends in Social Structure

V: Sociologists' interest in inequality in peasant, industrial, or advanced industrial societies has led them to make prolonged attempts to chart trends in social stratification. The notion of social class—either as a summary concept based on the consequences of the division of labor or induced from statistical measures—has to be utilized with the utmost caution. The accumulated scholarship on industrialization and urbanization in the eighteenth and nineteenth centuries underlines that "social class"—expressed in symbols such as the aristocracy, bourgeoisie, or working class—refers to categories of political debate as much as it does to the social realities in the system of stratification. Over the course of time, the language of political debate has influenced the concepts of social research.

It can be argued that with the intensification of urbanization and industrialization after the American and French revolutions it has become less and less useful to describe the social structure of the Western nation-state by means of a limited number of society-wide social strata (or classes) analogous to geological strata.[1] Such an analogy obscures the complexities of

---

[1]Lloyd A. Fallers, *Inequality: Social Stratification Reconsidered* (Chicago: University of Chicago Press, 1973).

contemporary industrial society. Sociologists must struggle to resist such oversimplified, schematic representations, since the patterns of social stratification are complex and rooted not only in socioeconomic position but also in age, sex, and religious differences, in ethnic-racial attachments, and in patterns of urban settlement.

Occupation and Inequality

As a result of such complexity, it is necessary to assert that the social stratification under the welfare state is best characterized as systems of inequality that, although overlapping, create a highly differentiated social structure. Instead of the imagery of two, four, or six society-wide social strata, the reality is an intricate pattern of social differentiation. An elaborate network of membership and participation in voluntary associations, plus social and cultural definitions reinforced by the mass media, serve to articulate these patterns of inequality. The result is hardly a collection of isolated individuals, a state of mass anomie, although a minority of persons have such features. Instead, we are dealing with a pattern of "ordered segmentation," and the central problem is the extent and nature of the articulation and disarticulation of these social segments.[2]

Nevertheless, it remains appropriate to use the occupational structure as a point of departure for describing the transformation of social structure and inequal-

---

[2]See Jerry Suttles, *The Social Order of the Slum* (Chicago: University of Chicago Press, 1968): Morris Janowitz and Jerry Suttles, "The Social Ecology of Citizenship" (forthcoming).

ity. Under the leadership of Otis Dudley Duncan and Albert J. Reiss, Jr., sociologists have carefully documented the increased occupational specialization of an advanced industrial society.[3] Their findings supply an empirical justification for Karl Mannheim's observation that with the growth of industrialization men and women come to think of themselves less as belonging to social classes and more as belonging to occupational and skill groupings. This is the direct effect of the process of urbanization and industrialization. The modern organization of work and the separation of work from family and residential life require a more and more elaborated system of socialization and social control, a system of education before entry to work, and an ongoing community and associational participation during adulthood.

As a result, social class, current level of income, and occupation categories do not serve effectively to identify life styles or mass political attitudes. Within the structure of social hierarchies and inequalities, family structure, educational experience, career patterns, and primordial attachments—real or constructed—plus community involvements, participation in voluntary associations, and exposure to the mass media become the essential elements in the complex system of social stratification and, accordingly, of the mechanisms of social control, effective and ineffective. It is not by accident that multivariate statistical analysis has become the standard procedure of analysis; this mode of analysis is appropriate for the changed social realities.

---

[3]Albert J. Reiss, Jr., Otis D. Duncan, Paul K. Hatt, and Cecil C. North, *Occupations and Social Status* (Glencoe, Ill.: The Free Press, 1962).

The literature of political sociology is replete with generalized observations that the more complex basis of social differentiation means a transformation in political conflict.[4] The political process and its manifested tension are not based, in this view, on broad social strata and social classes, which produce polarized political demands and action. Instead, the politics of an advanced industrial society is a reflection of its own system of inequality, which is characterized by intensive occupational and economic interest-group competition. This is hardly to assert the end of political conflict, as some have done; it is to emphasize that the thrust for a "revolutionary" seizure of the "organs of the state" yields to the goal of penetrating the parliamentary institutions.[5] "Revolutionary" politics has been traditionally constricted in the United States. Under advanced industrialism, the nature of political conflict has become a continuous and very explicit struggle of specific group interests.

The overriding consequence is political pressure through bargaining, direct political action, or even coercive tactics to achieve specific economic and legislative goals. The growth of the welfare state since 1945 represents less and less the influence of concep-

---

[4]For an exposition of the perspective of the "decline" of class-based political conflict and the "rise of consensus politics, see especially Seymour M. Lipset, "The Changing Class Structure and Contemporary European Politics," *Daedalus*, XCIII (Winter 1964): 271–303; Robert E. Lane, "The Politics of Consensus in an Age of Affluence," *American Political Science Review*, LIX (December 1965): 874–895. For the alternative view, which seeks to emphasize the emerging form of political conflict under advanced industrialism, see Morris Janowitz, *Political Conflict: Essays in Political Sociology* (Chicago: Quadrangle Books, 1970).

[5]Barrington Moore, Jr., "Revolution in America," *New York Review of Books*, XII (January 30, 1969): 6–12.

tualized goals—including class goals—and more and more the influence of the power of pressure-group politics reflecting the ordered segments of society, particularly those representing specific occupational groups.

National legislators, and more particularly the chief executive, become the central devices of social control for balancing, coordinating, and adjusting these competing demands but with declining effectiveness and constricted political legitimacy, especially in a period of chronic economic deficit. The overall level of expenditures is based less on a national conception of economic policy and more on the summation of competing pressures.

This view of occupational interest-group politics still implies that a person and the members of his household are linked to the larger society through the mechanism of the marketplace, that is, by the system of labor-commodity exchange under various forms of competition or monopoly. This is the contemporary view of the social relations generated by the mode of production. But the complexities of social stratification encompass more than the consequences of occupational differentiation; they rest on the social relations generated by the institutions of the welfare state, in addition to ordered segmentation reflecting race, ethnicity, religion, and local community attachments.

Consequences of Welfare Claims

In particular, the rise of the welfare state not only reflects the growth of urbanism and industrialism; it also serves as a mechanism for transforming the social structure and the patterns of social control. The pattern and magnitude of allocations of the welfare state become part of the system of inequality. A person and the members of his family are linked to the larger society by more than occupation and the mode of production that labor-commodity relations create. Their attachment to the larger society also reflects the effect of allocations of the welfare system that are based on transfers and grants created by the political and administrative apparatus.

There is a tendency in social research to treat these welfare allocations as exchanges. In this usage, the world "exchanges" is so broad and so generic as to have little meaning. In effect, it means little more than social relations. However, welfare transfers and allocations have their specific normative definitions. They are not gifts, for they involve a conflict of political values. The moral status of welfare is subject to the most intense debate and redefinition, precisely because welfare transactions are generated by a collective political act.

The social incidence and influence of the welfare system vary widely. The idea of the welfare state is based on the assumption that the lower social strata require additional resources. The emergence of the welfare state has produced a system that has as its official goals "assisting" those at the bottom of the social structure. But the long-term trend is one in which there is a diffusion of social welfare upward and throughout the social structure. In part, this is because the simplified and broad images of lower, middle, and upper social strata fail to encompass the real-life dilemmas of the populations of an advanced industrial society. Each additional dimension of social stratification or inequality of age, sex, and residence creates new and enlarged definitions for social welfare services.

For some, welfare becomes the sole source of sustenance throughout their entire lives; but they are a very small minority of the total population—and a minority of central moral consideration. More typically, welfare supplies crucial resources at a particular phase of a person's life cycle or a crucial supplement for a specific period of time. With all its imperfections and distortions, social welfare's normative rationale is based on aspirations for universal treatment and standards. Thus, such welfare operates in direct opposition to the particular rewards of occupation and work systems of exchange. As a result, the social stratification system is more than the existing distribution of occupation and associated skills. The classic question, "What are the consequences of the mode of production on the social structure?" has validity to the extent that it encompasses the consequences of the modalities of the social welfare system.

It makes sense to examine the impact of the welfare state on social stratification and inequality by focusing on the patterns of income and ownership of property and the resulting distribution of expendable resources. There is a body of data that focuses on the conclusion that during the expansion of the welfare state under the New Deal and throughout World War II income became more equally distributed and there was also a gradual reduction in the percentage of the population below the poverty line.[6] The extent to which this was the result of social welfare legislation and the extent to which it reflected the expansion of employment and increases in the level of economic productivity remain unknown. However, since 1950, further redistribution of income has not occurred. In other words, the marked growth of welfare transfer payments has not resulted in a greater degree of income equality; this was especially true during the period 1961 to 1970.[7] This is not to overlook the observation that the pattern of income distribution could have and would have been unequal without such increased transfers. (The stream of transfer income payments rose from $28.5 billion in 1960 to $158.8 billion in 1975.) No doubt this is because of the absence of more progressive taxation; but the income pattern also reflects the reduced level of economic development—for example, the rate of growth of economic productivity is lower in the United States than in Western Germany.

But the influence of the welfare state on the social structure and in turn on political participation and mass political opinion requires a broader approach than income distribution. This is especially so if one is to link changes in the social structure to social control by means of electoral behavior and the emergence of weak parliamentary majorities. It becomes necessary to encompass the full pattern of economic "equity

---

[6]Herman Miller, *Income Distribution in the United States* (Washington, D.C.: Department of Commerce, Bureau of the Census, 1966). Prepared for and in cooperation with the Social Science Research Council.
[7]Morgan Reynolds and Eugene Smolensky, "The Post F I S C Distribution: 1961 and 1970 Compared," *National Tax Journal,* XXVII (No. 4): 515–530.

claims"—private and public—and join those resulting from the marketplace with those being created by the intervention of the welfare state. "Equity claims" are the income and services that a person and the members of his family come to hold as accruing to him regardless of ownership of the capital resources involved. If the idea of equity claims is broadly defined, it becomes possible to speak of a "democratization" of economic equity. In this sense, democratization focuses less on equality of claims and more on the broadening of the base of participation in obtaining income benefits and services. The democratization of economic equity claims is a parallel of the extension of the franchise and other modes of political participation.

Two elements are involved. First, during the period of high economic growth of productivity after 1945, the economic surplus produced an increase in individual welfare schemes. Individuals decided to forego immediate consumption for investment to create long-term funds for medical expenses, children's educational benefits, and retirement benefits. Second, the intervention of the welfare state created new expectations of great magnitude and scope for benefits and services. As a result, it is obvious, but it must never for a moment be forgotten that under advanced industrialism the new pattern of equity claims blurs the distinction between wage earner and property owner. The surplus income of the postwar period has been used by individuals to create, for extensive segments of the society, economic reserves for their private welfare schemes. The major mechanism for such equity has been the widespread home ownership that began after World War I and was greatly extended after World War II. Home ownership penetrates deeply into modest- and even low-income families (except for the very lowest, it is almost unrelated to income). Home ownership by lower-income families has been facilitated by government-insured mortgages, which is a form of social welfare. In addition, private welfare has been enlarged by the diffusion of personal insurance policies and schemes, stock ownership, and supplementary pension plans based on the purchase of equity stock. While these devices hardly eliminate inequality, they have altered the linkages between wage earners and the mode of production. There is a shortage of adequate data on the incidence of these economic equity claims, but their widespread diffusion has been marked. It can be estimated that between one-third and one-half of the blue-collar families by the mid-1960s had such "stakes." However, it is the equity claims created by the welfare state, rather than these "capitalist" investments, that transform the basis of social stratification and inequality.

At the core of the welfare state are the income "maintenance" schemes, from old-age payments to rent supplements to food stamps. These programs penetrate well beyond the lowest social stratum. Thus, for example, over 100,000 members of the armed forces in the early 1970s were eligible to receive food stamps. Old-age insurance has become a crucial device for members of the middle strata to relieve themselves of or shift the burden of caring for their aging parents. Veterans' benefits are social welfare, since they are as much designed to overcome liabilities as they are to be rewards. The emerging programs of medical insurance are more and more broadly based. Significantly, elements of these programs are closely linked to the cost of living index.

Likewise, the dispersion of welfare equity claims received a powerful impetus from the extension of mass education. Expenditures for education produce high rates of economic return and influence a person's social position.[8] Since 1945, there has been massive extension of public support for higher education. University education is almost directly related to occupational position, and as a result these benefits serve to link the middle class—old and new—to the structure of the welfare state.

These data and the resulting effect of the welfare system on the social order supply the context for exploring the political consequences of the welfare state. Conventional political science is concerned with social stratification and interest-group politics and emphasizes the claims and demands of occupations articulated in terms of voluntary-associations networks. Each occupational group has a short-term but relatively stable interest that competes and conflicts with those of other groups. The inequality of contemporary society, the competition among interest groups, and the structure of political parties help account for the steady expansion of the welfare state. The political process is unable to impose a national scheme or an

---

[8]Theodore W. Schultz, *Investment in Human Capital: The Role of Education and of Research* (New York: The Free Press, 1971).

integrated economic policy and instead reacts by a series of compromises without "grand design" and without effective contribution to social control and self-regulation of the welfare state.

But the influence of the welfare state on the social structure modifies and transcends the format of conventional interest-group politics. Political conflict becomes more than the struggle between competing occupational and interest groups. Each person and each member of his household must confront an elaborated set of contradictory or competing and often ambiguous issues in the pursuit of his self-interest—immediate or long-term. The new social and economic structure produces a fusion of claims and expectations about wages, property income, and welfare claims. A person's linkages to the mode of production under these conditions is based both on his occupation and on the institutions of social welfare.

Of course, the claims and expectations of one's occupation remain central. However, the democratization of equity means that the return and stability of property rights, individual welfare plans, and the benefits of public social welfare are also crucial components for the citizenry at large. The task of assessing one's self-interest becomes continuous and more complex, and pursuing one's personal or group goals almost defies direct programmatic articulation. There is no reason to assume that a decline in political participation under such circumstances is the result; rather, a transformation of the forms, patterns, and consequences of political participation takes place. Traditional occupational interest-group politics produces relatively stable political attachments, which permit integrated preferences that shift slowly. It creates a political setting that has generated a form of bargaining politics by political leaders who can make fairly accurate assessments of popular demands and preferences. The arena of politics has consisted of large stable foci, and political competition has focused on segments of the electorate that shift gradually. The arena of political competition has had built-in and self-generating limits. The complex social base of political participation under the welfare state conditions new patterns of political involvement—patterns characterized by a high degree of volatility, which does not really lead to stable and unified political preferences and alliances and which helps account for the lack of clear-cut political majorities and the emergence of weak parliamentary regimes.

The Emergence
of Weak Political
Regimes

VI:

The difficulties of the welfare state contribute to the emergence of weak political regimes at the national level. The problem is not the personalities of the presidents or prime ministers in the Western political democracies but rather the inability of the electoral system to generate a decisive majority for one political organization or for an effective coalition. The narrow and unstable balance of power between legislative groupings, the opposition of chief executive to legislature members, the fragmentation of political factions—these difficulties are widespread in the Western industrialized nations and have been developing at least since the middle of the 1960s and in effect earlier, since the end of World War II.

It needs to be emphasized that this trend has emerged not only in the United States but throughout Western Europe. It is most conspicuous in Great Britain, the Netherlands, Belgium, and Denmark. It has been chronic in Italy and in varying degrees has come into being in Sweden and even in the Federal Republic of West Germany. France has its own tradition of chronic electoral instability, but the contemporary trend conforms to those of other Western industrialized nations.

Political parties and the periodic national elections are not able to perform the self-regulating tasks of social control. It is possible to examine and focus on the internal structure of the political parties, their social composition, their processes of leadership recruitment, their financial bases, and their internal decision-making process as elements in an explanation of this secular trend. While such an elite and institutional analysis helps clarify the weakness of contemporary parliamentary regimes, this analysis focuses on the changing character of the social structure.[1] The tensions and conflicts that the political elites and political organizations must confront reflect not only the altered mode of large-scale industrial production but also the development of the welfare expenditures managed by the state. In other words, the necessities of industrial development create the welfare state; and, in turn, the welfare state generates a set of economic equity claims that are complex, diffuse, and even mutually contradictory.

Moreover, welfare expenditures do not necessarily generate partisan loyalties. To the contrary, these allocations are more and more considered a matter of law and citizen right. This orientation serves to weaken or undermine partisan attachments.

The argument offered is that these welfare benefits change the patterns of social stratification and economic inequality, which in turn condition political participation and party orientation and help to explain the emergence of weak political regimes. Thus, popu-

---

[1]Elite dimensions are discussed in the epilogue.

lar electoral behavior can be taken as an index of social control, that is, voting patterns as indicators of the relative level of effectiveness of contemporary mechanisms of social and political control.

Critical Elections

One can assert that in the past socioeconomic change in the United States and the emergence of the welfare state created the need for political change. The political arrangements that facilitated industrial growth had to be adapted to the welfare state. The effectiveness of the process of adaptation and its limitations can be assessed by the key notion of the critical or realignment election. In the research literature, the elections of 1896 and 1932 are offered as such critical elections because they served to restructure political alternatives and produce important political decisions.[2] Three elements are operative in a critical election. First, the critical election produces a new majority—that is, there is a marked realignment in the sociopolitical basis of the majority and minority blocs. Second, the shift is sharp and relatively durable. Third, these two elements imply that the restructuring of the patterns of voting creates a decisive political majority, which has important and persistent political consequences. Thereby, the realignment election represents a decisive accomplishment in terms of self-regulation and

[2]V. O. Key, Jr., "A Theory of Critical Elections," *Journal of Politics,* XVII (February 1955): 3–18; W. D. Burnham, "The Changing Shape of the American Political Universe," *American Political Science Review,* LIV (March 1965): 7–28; W. D. Burnham, *Critical Elections and the Mainsprings of American Politics* (New York: Norton, 1970).

social control. Each occurrence of a critical election is apparently foreshadowed. This was so in the emergence of a "Populist" vote in 1894 in advance of the critical election of 1896. Again, the campaign of Alfred Smith represented the preliminary step in reorienting the Democratic party in 1928 and was the essential precondition for the Franklin D. Roosevelt political coalition of 1932 and thereafter.

It may well be that the passage of time and the limited empirical data help create, in retrospect, the image of a realignment election. Therefore, more time is required to identify the critical elections after 1932. However, in view of the weak political regimes that have emerged and the contemporary "crisis" of political legitimacy, there may well have been no subsequent critical election. Since 1945, there has been no critical election in the United States that has produced an effective and fairly enduring parliamentary majority in response to the emerging issues of the post-World War II period. Instead, there has been continuous, marginal, and unstable political aggregation. In other words, the election of 1932 was the last critical election. There is no reason to assume that another critical election will not take place, but the changes in the patterns of social stratification and inequality under the welfare state complicate the process of electoral transformation.

In any case, the concept of the critical election sets the historical framework for the trend analysis of the emergence of weak political regimes. For this purpose, the periods 1920 to 1948 and 1948 to 1972 are appropriate for comparison. In Table 8, the trends in United

TABLE 8
Trends in Political Participation and Political Mandate in United States National Elections, 1920–1972

YEAR	TURNOUT PRESIDENTIAL ELECTION (PERCENT)	PRESIDENT	PRESIDENTIAL MANDATE POPULAR VOTE PLURALITY (PERCENT OF TURNOUT)	LEGISLATIVE MANDATE HOUSE OF REPRESENTATIVES PLURALITY (NO. OF SEATS)	SENATE PLURALITY (NO. OF SEATS)
1920	44.0	Harding	Rep. 26.3	169	23
1924	44.0	Coolidge	Rep. 25.2	14	10
1928	52.0	Hoover	Rep. 17.3	38	5
1932	52.4	Roosevelt	Dem. 17.7	193	25
1936	56.9	Roosevelt	Dem. 24.3	242	50
1940	58.9	Roosevelt	Dem. 9.9	106	38
1944	56.0	Roosevelt	Dem. 7.5	52	18
1948	51.1	Truman	Dem. 4.5	92	2
1952	61.6	Eisenhower	Rep. 10.7	0	1
1956	59.3	Eisenhower	Rep. 15.4	-33	-2
1960	62.8	Kennedy	Dem. 0.2	89	30
1964	61.8	Johnson	Dem. 22.7	145	36
1968	60.9	Nixon	Rep. 0.7	-51	-14
1972	55.7	Nixon	Rep. 23.2	-47	-14

States national elections are presented in a fashion designed to highlight the changing morphology of voting patterns and the type and strength of the political majority that emerged.

To work effectively, a competitive election must create a stable majority that is able to rule. The balance between the majority and the minority must be such that the minority—by itself or in coalition with other political elements—maintains a reasonable chance of success in forthcoming elections. If the majority becomes excessively preponderant, viability of the electoral system as a mechanism of self-regulation is weakened. But the opposite situation has come to characterize the pattern of electoral behavior both in the United States and generally in Western Europe. The outcome of the national election, in one form or another, is such that an effective and stable political regime is not created. There has been a growth of "weak," or minority, governments. The forms and patterns are diverse. The margin of victory for the leading party may be slim; or, in fact, the victorious party may obtain only a minority of the vote; likewise, its parliamentary majority may be too narrow to be considered a governing party. In the presidential system, the chief executive may find himself with the opposition party in command of the legislative majority. The result of these outcomes is hardly an effective system of checks and balances; rather it is political fragmentation or disarticulation and a variety of forms of stalemate, because there has not been a critical or realignment election which has constructed an effective political majority.

For the United States, in the period 1920 to 1928, the electoral system created a relatively stable majority political regime that was Republican and that endured for three presidential terms. It was replaced in 1932 by a stable Democratic majority political regime, which persisted for an even longer period of time, namely five presidential terms. However, since 1948 the outcome has been neither a relatively stable political regime nor, with one single exception in 1964, even a single term of control of both the Presidency and both legislative houses by the same party; instead, the results have been disarticulated.

While the political historians do not identify the post-World War I election of 1920 as a critical election, it did replace the Wilson administration and create a Republican majority that persisted until 1932. The electoral competition gave the Republican presidents decisive popular mandates (ranging from an advantage of 26.3 percent in 1920 to 7.3 percent in 1928); moreover, these presidents had working majorities in both houses of Congress throughout the period.

In 1928, the first element of a movement toward a critical election could be seen—that is, seen in retrospect. The drop in the popular vote for the President was noteworthy but limited; it was the decline in senatorial seats for the Republicans that signaled the emergence of the new Democratic party with its new strength and base in the North. The 1932 election has been defined by political historians as a critical election because it created the new Democratic party majority, a decisive majority, which persisted both in the popular vote for the President and in the composition of both houses of Congress. The high point was reached in 1936 when Roosevelt gained a plurality of 24.3 percent. The trend in the popular presidential majority was consistently downward after 1936 but still reached 7.5 percent in 1944. The popular Democratic presidential position was paralleled by a consistent majority in both houses, which was tempered at critical points because of the importance of the North-South political split. However, from 1920 through the election of 1944 the electoral system created relatively clear-cut political regimes.

In retrospect, the election of 1948 had the elements of an election antecedent to a critical election of realignment. The popular advantage of the Democratic president continued to decline; it reached the level of 4.5 percent. While the House of Representatives returned a decisive majority of Democratic legislators, the majority in the Senate was reduced to two members. The elements of emerging political disarticulation were beginning to appear.

The outcome of the 1952 election was not that of a critical election of realignment. Instead, the post-World War II pattern of executive dominance—unstable dominance at that—and a stalemated or divided legislative balance emerged. In contrast to the majority political regimes of the period 1920 to 1944, the elements of the "weak" system of parliamentary rule had their origins not in the particular political events of the 1968 to 1972 period but in the results already foreshadowed in the election of 1952. The long-term trend from 1952 to 1972 can be described in part as a period of decline in the national legislative strength of the Republican party. However, we are dealing with more than the relative electorate strength of the major parties. We are dealing with basic changes in the structure of electoral behavior.

In 1952, General Dwight D. Eisenhower was elected by a decisive majority (10.7 percent advantage) but not by a margin of the magnitude accorded Republican presidents in the post-World War I period or to Roosevelt in the first two elections of the New Deal period. Moreover, Eisenhower did not have a formal (and certainly not a working) majority in the legislature as a whole. The distribution was balanced in the House of Representatives, and the number of Republican senators only exceeded the number of Democrats by one. For the first time since 1920, the United States government was not based on a unified political regime. In 1956, General Eisenhower increased his popular vote so that the percent advantage reached 15.4 percent; but the pattern of unstable disarticulation was becoming institutionalized. In both houses of Congress, the Democratic party was in the formal majority—with only 2 seats more than the Republicans in the Senate, but more markedly in the House of Representatives with 33 seats more. The weak government in the United States is not the result of the Vietnam era but has been operative increasingly throughout the post-World War II period.

The pattern of national elections continued essentially in this format through the 1972 election. In 1960, the Democratic president was elected without an effective popular mandate, although he had a working majority in both houses of Congress (30 in the Senate, and 89 in the House of Representatives). Only in the 1964 election did Lyndon B. Johnson create the conventional pre-World War II majority political regime with a landslide popular mandate and a marked increase in the Democratic majority in both houses of Congress. However, the result of the 1964 election could not be taken as a critical election of realignment since by 1968 Richard Nixon was elected as the head of a minority political regime. He collected only a plurality of the popular presidential vote (43.4 percent) and his advantage over the Democratic candidate was limited to 0.7 percent. The strength of the George Wallace vote, which totaled 13.6 percent of the vote, rendered him, in effect, a minority president. Moreover, the Democratic party held a working majority in both houses of Congress (14 in the Senate and 51 in the House of Representatives). The pattern of a divided political regime or a disarticulated outcome was even more pronounced in the 1972 election in which Richard Nixon achieved a landslide popular majority—a 23.2 percent advantage over the Democratic contender—but the dominance of the Democratic legislators in both houses of Congress remained.

The implications for the social control perspective are clear. If one assumes that the election outcome is a manifestation of the relative ability of a society to regulate itself, then the absence of a stable majority political regime implies that this indicator reflects significant limitations in the patterns of effective control. Moreover, the election is more than an indicator of social control—it is a mechanism for achieving social control. Thus, these data highlight the strain on the central institution for implementing effective social control.

Trends in Electoral Behavior

The available data on citizens' participation in the national elections help clarify the emergence of weak political regimes. Four specific trends in electoral participation can be examined which extend from 1920 to 1975 and highlight the transformation of electoral participation. The patterns of transformation give meaning to the increasing inability of the electoral process since the election of 1948 to generate stable and majority political regimes. We are dealing with relatively long-term trends and not the particular manifestation of the elections of 1968 and 1972. These specific trends deal with (*a*) the level of voting participation, (*b*) fluctuations in voting preference, (*c*) shifts in patterns of party affiliation, and (*d*) beliefs about the legitimacy and effectiveness of the electoral process and elected officials. As in the analysis of critical elections, the election of 1952 is a useful dividing point for the period after 1920.

First, the trend in voting participation indicates that since 1952 the long-term increase after the turn of the century has not effectively maintained. Given the increasing levels of education, wide exposure to the mass media, and the politicization of minority groups, the failure of voting participation to increase is particularly noteworthy. During the period after 1920 and especially after 1930, competitive politics directly influenced the turnout and increased voting participation. The trend is not consistently upward, since in 1944 and 1948 the turnout failed to reach the level reached in 1940. In terms of secular trends, the election of 1952 produced one high point in the presidential turnout. Since 1952, the new pattern of a disarticulated political result in the national election has been accompanied by no further increases in voting participation. In fact, from 1952 to 1968 the overall turnout remained fairly stable (varying from 59 to 62 percent), while in the election campaign of 1972 between Richard Nixon and George McGovern, voter participation dropped markedly to 55.7 percent. Thus, from 1960 to 1972 and especially in 1972 in the United States, competitive politics, which remained intense, did not produce increased levels of electoral participation.

Second, since 1952 there has been an increase in the magnitude of shifts in voting patterns from one election to the next. In other words, the post-World War II period has not been characterized by a system composed of large voting blocs with the outcome, from one election to the next, being determined by rather small shifts in voter preference. To the contrary, the structure of the electorate reveals an increasingly important segment that is prepared to shift from one pattern of voting to another with its members changing their preference for president and engaging in an increasing amount of ticket splitting. Higher levels of education and more extensive political sophistication as a result of the mass media facilitate this trend. But the underlying explanation must be sought in the changing social basis of political participation and the citizens' resulting definition of their political self-interest.

If one examines the period from 1920 to 1948, omitting the realignment election of 1932, one finds that the pattern of voting shifts from one election to the next is moderate. The average two-party shift for the six presidential elections was 5.0 percentage points. However, from 1948 to 1972 electoral behavior was much more volatile. In fact, the average two-party shift was three times as great. For the seven presidential elections, the average shift was 17.1 percentage points.

Along with increased volatility, there has been a growth in ticket splitting. The documentation showing this trend is indeed impressive. Paul T. David has demonstrated the continuous and persistent increase in ticket splitting from 1872 to 1970.[3] His analysis is based on the difference in six pairs of voting decisions involving the offices of president, governor, senator, and representatives. It is striking that there is no reversal in the long-term trend of a century in the increased ticket splitting.

Third, the number of citizens who describe themselves as independents or as having no basic party affiliation has increased since 1952, and especially among young voters. The specific observation that there has been a shift in the characteristics of those citizens who call themselves independent is especially important. As of 1952, the bulk of the independents had weak involvements in politics and marginal political preferences. The trend has been one in which independents are increasingly persons with more education and with strong interests in politics and articulated political demands. Thus, the growth of the concentra-

---

[3]Paul T. David, *Party Strength in the United States, 1872–1970* (Charlottesville, Va: University Press of Virginia, 1972).

tion of independents does not imply a decline in political interest and involvement, since an important number of them think of themselves as politically responsible and involved.[4]

According to Gallup surveys, the trend in the electorate of those who consider themselves independents ranges from a low of 20 percent in 1940 to 34 percent in 1974. From October 1952 to November 1970, the findings of the Survey Research Center, University of Michigan, confirm these trends. Both these sources also point out that the trend toward "independent" affiliation is even more pronounced among young people. In fact, among college students, by 1974 almost one-half called themselves independents.

Fourth, since 1964 there has been a trend toward a marked reduction in trust and confidence in the electoral system and the outcome of elections. This trend is no doubt linked to the specific impact of military intervention in Vietnam and has been strengthened by the events surrounding the Watergate investigation. However, it antedates the first years of the 1970s and reflects underlying changes in the social structure and in the organization of politics.[5]

None of these trends can be taken as a measure per se of political apathy or depoliticization of the citizens of the United States; they are manifestations of the tension between political goals and available political means. They reflect underlying changes in social

[4]Philip E. Converse, "Change in the American Electorate," in Angus Campbell and Philip E. Converse, eds., *The Human Meaning of Social Change* (New York: Russell Sage Foundation, 1972), pp. 263–338.
[5]Ibid., pp. 322–330.

stratification and inequality and the ineffectiveness of the political process as a mechanism of social control. In particular, these electoral trends highlight the long-term pattern of attenuation of stable affiliation with the two major parties. In the absence of decisive electoral realignments, extraparliamentary mechanisms for social control of the welfare state become of increasing importance. Nevertheless, whether one charts long-term trends in electoral participation and attitudes or uses the notion of critical elections, the emergence of weak political regimes (in the United States and in the nations of Western Europe) is significantly conditioned by changes in social stratification and patterns of inequality created by the expansion of the welfare state.[6] In other words, it is the combined impact of the shifts in social stratification plus the impact of a welfare budget based on the decline of economic surplus that strains the electoral and parliamentary institutions.

---

[6]The extensive use of public opinion polling has not served to strengthen the electoral process as some experts had anticipated. The results of surveys have been to frame issues in such a fashion as to fragment the electoral process rather than to encourage public concern with the coherence and legitimacy of contending political parties. Surveys create the impression in segments of the citizenry of mass manipulation as well and serve at times to shift the context from competition about issues to that between personalities. Mark Abrams, "Political Parties and the Polls," in Paul F. Lazarsfeld, William H. Sewell, and Harold L. Wilensky, eds., *The Uses of Sociology* (New York: Basic Books, 1967), pp. 427–436.

The Psychological
Context of Welfare

VII:
It is appropriate to speculate about the psychology of the welfare state. The psychological effect of welfare schemes becomes a topic for tough-minded speculation. How can the consequences of welfare institutions be separated from the analysis of the more general influence of industrial and modern institutions? In addition, how does one examine the issue of the impact of modern war—and particularly the threat of nuclear destruction, which supplies the overriding context—a topic that cannot be said to have produced pointed research conclusions?

But the student of the difficulties of the welfare state and its mechanisms of social control can use three bodies of research: (a) the massive body of attitude studies that chart public opinion about politics and the agencies of government; (b) the body of literature that deals with the process of socialization of personality, especially that aspect that has come to stress the centrality of cognitive processes; and (c) the quantitative studies of self-destructive and deviant behavior.

Over the last quarter of a century, social research has made enormous efforts to use the sample survey to examine the structure of social attitudes under advanced industrialism. These efforts have been persistently criticized by writers like Herbert Blumer as using an individualist and mechanistic methodology, which gives their findings little analytic relevance. However, over the years this type of criticism has atrophied, from an intellectual point of view. It is impossible to think of contemporary analysis of social organization and political behavior, as well as collective psychology, without recourse to the massive and continuously collected survey and public opinion data. Sociologists with diverse policy perspectives, such as S. M. Lipset and Richard F. Hamilton, demonstrate their joint commitment to reliance on the sample survey for their analysis of attitudes about political authority and issues.[1]

However, a profound paradox is involved in utilizing the sample survey to highlight the psychological context of the welfare state. The central relevance of the sample survey rests on its ability to chart changes in attitudes over time. But university-based sample surveys have essentially been used for ad hoc investigation of specific topics, and only in recent years has there been increased attention to trend data on social attitudes collected by means of sample surveys. Thus, Angus Campbell and Philip Converse's effort to synthesize available findings under the title *Human Consequences of Social Change* could present a comprehensive set of indicators of changes in attitudes about life chances and the expanded institutions of so-

---

[1]S. M. Lipset and Earl Raab, *The Politics of Unreason: Right-Wing Extremism in America, 1890–1970* (New York: Harper and Row, 1970); Richard F. Hamilton, *Class and Politics in the United States* (New York: Wiley, 1972).

cial welfare.[2] The most penetrating analysis of pertinent social attitudes about the effect of the welfare state is contained in W. G. Runciman's cross-sectional study *Social Justice and Relative Deprivation,* which seeks to explore the extent to which existing inequalities are viewed as legitimate by the British population.[3]

However, from the available survey data one can piece together measures about satisfaction with life chances and associated attitudes about the social order. As could have been expected, the emergence of stagflation, since 1970, has contributed to increased levels of personal discontent, less optimism about the welfare of one's children, and a decline in confidence and trust in the institutions of government. However, long-term trend data about intergroup attitudes and levels of prejudice warrant close attention. The tensions of advanced industrialism have been accompanied by continuous decline in prejudice toward minority groups, even during the period of racial disturbance and the subsequent impact of stagflation.[4] It remains to be assessed whether these attitudes reflect tolerance or just studied indifference. But the inference is that the institutions of social welfare serve to

---

[2] Angus Campbell and Philip Converse, eds., *The Human Meaning of Social Change* (New York: Russell Sage Foundation, 1972).
[3] W. G. Runciman, *Relative Deprivation and Social Justice: A Study of Attitudes to Social Inequality in Twentieth-Century England* (Berkeley, Calif.: University of California Press, 1966). See also Michael Schiltz, *Public Attitude toward Social Security, 1935–1965* (Washington, D.C.: Social Security Administration, Office of Research and Statistics, 1970).
[4] Bruno Bettelheim and Morris Janowitz, *Social Change and Prejudice* (New York: The Free Press, 1975).

inhibit potential negative psychological impacts in this crucial regard.

Likewise, the research literature on socialization presents suggestive but fragmented insights into the patterns of social control under the welfare state. One central stream in this literature has emphasized the cognitive aspects of the socialization process rather than the emotive and unconscious process of human development. This emphasis has involved the formulation of models of human potentials—a shift reflecting the short-term economic productivity and abundance immediately after World War II. The lasting consequence of this form of psychological optimism has hardly been intellectually profound. The psychologist Jerome Bruner has been the leading spokesman for this perspective.[5] He has sought to reject the formulation of Jean Piaget, who focused on the development sequences of maturation. Instead, Bruner has offered this formulation, "We begin with the hypothesis that any subject can be taught effectively in some intellectually honest form to any child at any state of development." Such an assertion is patently not a hypothesis but a moral exhortation, since it rests on the crucial and completely ambiguous, or rather undefined, word "honest." The Bruner model had, for the moment, a strong influence on the American educational system with the proposition that early emphasis on cognitive skills would solve the "tough" questions of the socialization of mature, competent, and self-directed

[5]Jerome Bruner, *The Process of Education* (Cambridge, Mass.: Harvard University Press, 1960).

adults. This period, epitomized by the social movement of the new math and the "new curriculum," came quickly to an end under the impact of racial and student unrest.

Instead of a rigid cognitive approach to socialization, a broad and more comprehensive perspective—the institutional orientation—to the issues of socialization appears to have more enduring relevance. James Coleman and his study group have summarized the profound discontinuities associated with the transition from adolescence to adulthood in United States society.[6] They have focused on the narrow pathways mainly associated with academic performance in secondary school and the tensions that result from such overspecialization. The effective process of socialization, from this perspective, was asserted to rest on the combination of the academic with work experiences—in the fashion postulated by John Dewey over fifty years ago. While the ineffective process of youth socialization is concentrated in lower-income groups, the basic disarticulation extends throughout the entire social structure. In *Institution Building in Urban Education*, this author has analyzed the existing organization structure of mass education, which is seen as tending to differentiate the school from the urban environment and which internally operates on a fragmented basis because of the extreme specialization of its personnel.[7] Thus, the influence of advanced indus-

[6]James S. Coleman, et al., *Youth: Transition to Adulthood: Report of the Panel on Youth of the President's Science Advisory Committee* (Chicago: University of Chicago Press, 1974).
[7]Morris Janowitz, *Institution Building in Urban Education* (Chicago: University of Chicago Press, 1971).

trialization operates through educational institutions that are limited in their capacity to perform academic functions and to link academic goals to the broader goals of youth socialization.

The research literature on the impact of social welfare institutions is more descriptive and less oriented to the analytical considerations encountered in the study of public education. Nevertheless, the same organizational processes appear. Whether one is dealing with the format of public housing or with welfare services associated with family assistance programs and community development, the overall effect on the process of socialization is to separate and in fact isolate the clients from the larger social structure and to seek to treat their needs in a very fragmented fashion. While these programs have eliminated the stark misery of oppressive poverty and the fear of starvation, they contain strong built-in limitations that thwart self-esteem and competence among recipients.

But speculation about the psychological context of the welfare state requires a perspective that goes beyond the social attitudes and even the institutional dimensions of socialization. We are dealing in essence with the most generic aspects of personality and their relations to the welfare state. Social welfare concepts and programs as they have developed in the United States—and even in societies with a strong democratic socialist tradition—emphasize strengthening benefits and welfare rights on an individual basis. The welfare state is a strategy for making use of collective symbols and practices to achieve goals that are cast in an individualist mold. Thus, the welfare state is an extension of the main lines of liberal democracy that are embodied in the political aspirations of the Western nation-state.

Material Conditions and Hedonism

It may well be that Sigmund Freud's argument in *Civilization and Its Discontents* and *Beyond the Pleasure Principle* supplies the underlying assumption for the exploration of these psychological dimensions of the welfare state.[8] The argument rests on the idea that social welfare has produced the same, or at least converging, psychological responses of frustration as those generated by the material and cultural accumulations of industrial civilization. The impact of civilization renders it more difficult and more complex to pursue "instinctually" grounded pleasure and gratification. One chief characteristic of the affluent society is that it creates a heightened sensitivity or drive for hedonism—it produces, if you will, a concern with raw hedonism. The pursuit of hedonism—and raw hedonism—takes place in the context of ineffective and weak limits on personal control and of self-indulgence. We are dealing not only with the dimension of moral restraints but also with the decline of stylized forms of ritual and ceremony.

The pursuit of hedonism and of impulse gratification under these circumstances becomes difficult to mod-

---

[8]Sigmund Freud, trans. Jean Riviere, *Civilization and Its Discontents* (New York: J. Cape and H. Smith, 1930). Freud, trans. C. J. M. Hubback, *Beyond the Pleasure Principle* (London: The International Psycho-analytical Press, 1922).

erate and instead becomes more obsessive. The consequences of the heightened drive for hedonistic gratification in the absence of effective patterns of personal social control are distorted personal response and, fundamentally, an increase in unhappiness. The argument of Sigmund Freud parallels, as has been repeatedly pointed out, that presented by Emile Durkheim in *Le Suicide*.[9]

The admixture of increased material resources and changed normative values sets the context for the institutions of social welfare. The causes of human unhappiness are linked to those elements in the normative structure that emphasize the moral desirability of indulgence and gratification without creating a patterned structure of limits. This argument implies that the psychological distortion is exacerbated by the emphasis placed on the individual as the central judge of his psychic well-being rather than on the development of group standards and norms.

The issue can be stated in alternative terms. In modern society, there is a constant need for institutional efforts to define, redefine, and elaborate moral standards for behavior linked to personal gratification. For example, this is the role of the courts in elaborating the law. But in the drive for hedonism, the experience itself emerges as the central mechanism. The result must of necessity produce unhappiness for the individual person who is not supported by a network of intimate social relations that supply some normative standards about personal gratification.

It is indeed striking that in the 1960s the subject of

---

[9]Emile Durkheim, *Le Suicide* (Paris: F. Alcan, 1897).

happiness itself became the topic of empirical research.[10] The direct empirical assault on the subject has demonstrated that it is elusive. There is no body of trend data to indicate that higher standards of living have produced a discernible increase in measurable "happiness." If anything, the contrary appears to be the case.

Sociologists have also assaulted the issue because of their immense commitment to the study of deviant behavior. Confronted by the increased intensity in the pursuit of hedonistic indulgence, many have sought to explore the sociological and psychological dimensions of pleasure by asserting that the definitions of deviant behavior are arbitrary.[11] One can speak of the spread and diffusion or the "democratization" of hedonism and deviant behavior. The full capacity of the human being for indulgence and gratification requires, from this perspective, an examination of his ability to circumvent the arbitrary barriers of an advanced industrial society and to uncover the real sources of gratification. But highly relativistic sociologists cannot overlook the point at which the behavior involved in the search for gratification becomes a self-destructive response.

As measured by overt behavior and not by psychic states, there have been two long-term trends, revealed by available research, during the emergence of the welfare state since 1945. First, there has been a steady

---

[10]Norman Bradburn and David Caplovitz, *Reports on Happiness: A Pilot Study of Behavior Related to Mental Health* (Chicago: Aldine, 1965).
[11]Howard Becker, *Outsiders: Studies in the Sociology of Deviance* (New York: The Free Press of Glencoe, 1963).

increase in behavior that reflects the intensified drive for hedonistic gratification. This trend rests on increased affluence. The social indicators involve the increased per capita consumption of alcohol, tobacco, and drugs. There has also been a documented "quantitative" increase of sexual behavior. Second, for each of these overt pursuits of pleasure there has been an increase in the forms of behavior—deviant and otherwise—that must be labeled as self-destructive, without recourse to subtle moral, cultural, or political definitions. In addition to the indicators reflecting these particular indulgences, the central indicator of personal and social control remains, as for Durkheim, suicide, with its long-term increase and particularly among youth and minority groups. The joint operation of these trends emphasizes the argument of *Beyond the Pleasure Principle*. While the level of welfare for important segments of recipients leads to no more than a marginal existence, the long-term thrust of the system—actual and potential, with its direct and indirect effects—serves only to integrate the welfare recipient into the ineffective social control system of the larger society.

There are, of course, trends of varying strength and pervasiveness counter to self-centered hedonism. A tiny fraction of persons seek classic or modified forms of psychotherapy. The demand for therapy has increased with the spread of mass education and of social welfare institutions, and the welfare state does make some forms of psychotherapy available to submerged groups. The approaches required to adapt psychotherapy to the bureaucratized institutions of welfare remain problematic. Of particular importance has been the rapid emergence of the numerous forms of regressive therapy. (The basic criterion for judging regressive therapy is the likelihood of a damaging impact or a weakening effect on the ego's functions.) Through these forms, this therapy—which is not in reality "therapy"—becomes a further source of distorted and unsatisfactory pursuit "beyond the pleasure principle."[12] Likewise, the drive toward self-indulgence produces a variety of reaction formations in the society at large. Of particular note are the new intense, if fragile, group solidarities, the modern forms of "communalism." In these groups, the individual submerges his self-preoccupation on the basis of opposition to existing mores. The degree of personal commitment that is mobilized is deep and almost fearful. The "rationalistic" advanced industrial society generates its forms of communes—rural and urban—its student groups, its religious movements, and its semisecret formations. It may well be that these are movements of limited viability. There is a point at which they serve neither individual nor social needs, and the individual departs. In a society with great geographical mobility and elaborate role transitions, participation in these forms of "communion" may well be limited in duration for many. But these are psychological constructions of welfare, since these efforts will eventually have their influence on the broader institutions of contemporary society.

---

[12]Kurt W. Back, *Beyond Words: The Story of Sensitivity Training and the Encounter Movement* (New York: Russell Sage Foundation, 1973).

Institution Building
in Social Welfare

VIII:
There can be no doubt
that in the United States an increase in the expenditures for social welfare—particularly in the area of income maintenance—is required in order to ensure minimum standards of human dignity. Increased expenditures are necessary as an expression of the moral commitment of the larger society, and such expenditures serve to maintain the social base of a political democracy. The recommendations embodied in the 1974 report prepared for the Joint Economic Committee of the Congress of the United States under the leadership of Representative Martha W. Griffiths supply a measure of the increase required as of that year.[1] The restructuring of social welfare for income maintenance that was proposed would have cost about an additional $15 to $20 billion annually, at the then existing prices. In terms of the total gross national product, that goal does not seem utopian, and it hardly represents a confiscatory level of personal taxation. For a society that values personal and political freedom, there is clearly a level of taxation that has poten-

---

[1]Congress of the United States, Joint Economic Committee, Subcommittee on Fiscal Policy, *Income Security for Americans: Recommendations of the Public Welfare Study* (Washington: U.S. Government Printing Office, 1974).

tial negative consequences on personal incentives and on the legitimacy of the taxation system as a whole. Under advanced industrialism taxes that are viewed as excessively high are initially less likely to produce violent protest and more likely to result in loss of confidence and negativism toward the political institution and the system of social control. The reduction of the level of unemployment to below 5 percent would be essential for such a program.

But this analysis of the dilemmas of the welfare state implies that increases in welfare expenditures in the context of a "negative economic surplus" will not necessarily accomplish the task of decisively reducing human misery. Moreover, the logic of the welfare state requires that transformation be incremental. In the broadest terms, for effective social control, social welfare needs operate to meet criteria that are universalistic by the standards of contemporary society. Perhaps it is appropriate to assert that social welfare should create more nearly universal standards and operating procedures.

Of course, the reconstruction of social welfare is in good measure normative. In the nineteenth century, charity gave way to social welfare as an element of the individual citizen's rights. The current transformation deals with the social control of the system as a whole. In the most fundamental sense, the rights and benefits of social welfare are not to be argued in terms of the needs of particular individuals or specific classes of social groups. To the contrary, the moral criteria are those of distributive justice. The system of social welfare is designed to overcome personal and societal defects in order to make the social system operative and to produce effective social control. Therefore, for each social welfare problem, one must ask the question, "What is the situation of 'similar people' and how are they treated?" Social welfare—public and private, professionally managed and self-help–oriented—becomes an aspect of the overall social structure. It should not create thereby a distinct status group or stratum in society. But the transformation of social welfare in this direction is not to be conceived as solely or even primarily a normative issue; it requires a concern with organizational adaptation, that is, realistic "institution building."

The dilemmas of the welfare state under a parliamentary regime lead to three central issues in institution building. The first centers on the political economy of the system of the welfare state, both the mechanisms of labor-management bargaining and the governmental process of making welfare allocations. The second encompasses the modification of the structure of welfare institutions in order to eliminate the pervasive fragmentation and to improve the focus, effectiveness, and quality of services. The third deals with the psychological quality and effect of the welfare state, that is, with the matters of reconstructing the idea of the "therapeutic," in order to confront the psychological discontent of an advanced industrial society.

The issues at hand are posed as those of conceptual explication rather than as strategies for mobilization of support and consent. Social control under a welfare state requires institutional mechanisms for making effective and authoritative decisions with a minimum of coercion. The perspective of social control with which this analysis was launched and with which it concludes is that of a thrust to strengthen the modes of participation in the decision-making processes. The standing formula for analyzing the welfare state has appropriately been that of political sociology: "Who gets what, when, and how?" Such a formula focuses on existing political struggles and difficulties, but it is not a substitute for a policy orientation. The underlying objective of a social control perspective on welfare is to establish the appropriate criteria concerning "who should participate in what decision" if the welfare state is to function with effectiveness and under parliamentary control.

The technological and organizational bases of an advanced industrial society create pressures for extensive citizen participation. But there are advanced industrial societies without valid citizen participation and without competitive elections. The achievement of parliamentary institutions is not the automatic result of industrial and economic factors but of the consequence of political aspirations and accomplishments. The term "mass society" becomes relevant for the contemporary definition of this historic process.[2] "Mass society" means that each person considers himself to be a citizen because he has meaningful access to the political center of society and he is an integral part of the sociopolitical process.

By the first half of the nineteenth century, the aspi-

---

[2]Edward A. Shils, "The Theory of the Mass Society," *Diogenes*, No. 39 (1962): 45–66.

ration for fundamental democratization, in this respect, had become a powerful reality—to use again the phrase of Karl Mannheim.[3] In particular, he was referring to the political system that rested on universal suffrage as the key mechanism of integrating the individual into the citizen role. It was not until World War I in Great Britain and the civil rights movement in the 1960s in the United States that the institutional barriers to effective participation were fundamentally shaken. It still remains for the welfare state to make these rights effective and meaningful.

Of course, fundamental democratization carries with it the danger that the electoral system can be perverted into a mass plebiscitary movement. Karl Mannheim was writing in the shadow of the rise of National Socialism. The potential rise to power of extremist movements by means of the electoral process is never to be overlooked. However, this analysis of the effect of the welfare state asserts a changed vulnerability of mass democratic political institutions. A crisis like the Great Depression, which produced antidemocratic movements, gives way to the perpetual crisis that undermines political legitimacy and political confidence. As Barrington Moore, Jr., has emphasized, the outcome is less likely to be a revolutionary seizure of power and more likely to be a chronic state of tension and social ineffectiveness.[4]

In particular, the system of national and periodic elections is unable to produce the required parliamen-

[3]Karl Mannheim, *Man and Society in an Age of Reconstruction* (London: Kegan Paul, 1940).
[4]Barrington Moore, Jr., "Revolution in America," *New York Review of Books*, XII (January 30, 1969): 6–12.

tary majority. Resource allocation both for economic growth and for social welfare cannot be effected on a consistent basis. The political regime is unable to respond to the problems of the new economics.[5] Nonetheless, the national electoral system remains the central mechanism of social control in a parliamentary regime. The required thrust of institution building rests on the development of new procedures and mechanisms for the social control of the national economic accounts and in turn the development of citizen participation, which will directly and indirectly contribute to the effectiveness of the national electoral process.

There is no need to reproduce or to extend mechanically the procedures of a political election to all institutional sectors. Instead, the goal of institution building should be appropriate for each sector of society. As indicated above, from the point of view of social wel-

----

[5]It can be argued that there is no "new economics." The economies of the Western parliamentary nations are continuing to display their traditional capitalist characteristics. The recession-depression of 1973 to 1975 is no more than a continuation of capitalist economic instability. Periodic recession-depressions are required, especially in nations with high degrees of concentration of ownership, which undermines competition. Periodic recession-depressions enable large-scale industry to maintain their profits and impose discipline on the labor market. Such an analysis does not appear to fit the economic and political realities of these advanced industrial societies. First, the long-term profitability of invested capital continues to decline in the United States, and it is not improved by recession-depressions. Economists disagree on this issue, but the weight of available evidence supports this conclusion. Two, there is no evidence that recession-depressions in the absence of modification of labor-management relations restore labor discipline or in many circumstances necessarily modulate inflationary wage demands. Third, recession-depressions do not arrest the trend toward the expansion of the welfare state but, rather, accelerate it. Fourth, to the extent that conscious management preferences operate, industrial managers prefer gradual expansion policies rather than "boom and bust" cycles.

fare the first step is to explore institution building in regard to the management of the national accounts in order to deal with the persistent deficit financing of social welfare expenditures and the difficulties of making allocations between competing claims.

National Economic Accounts

The economics of social welfare is based on a system of national accounts. The existing economic categories with their arbitrary dimensions define the reality of chronic budget deficits and set the parameters for alternative economic policy. The goals of economic policy for the welfare state are to reduce unemployment, increase productivity (and this requires increased investments), and modulate the long-term rate of inflation (to the level of 5 percent annually).

It is impossible to rely on either the fiscalist or the monetarist approach to achieve these objectives. First, there is insufficient theoretical and empirical evidence for a decisive acceptance of one alternative over the other. Second, in fact, the state of economic theory is such that professional economists of the highest repute are prepared to maintain that both policies can be pursued simultaneously. In actual application the crucial difference between the alternative approaches becomes a matter of emphasis and therefore of professional judgment. Third, each point of view assumes the existence of more effective levels of social control. The goals that both seek imply their prior existence if their policies are to be effective. To pursue the monetarist approach to control inflation would require a higher level of unemployment than is tolerable or acceptable under existing political norms. There must be an operative mechanism, such as a negative income tax, that is not institutionalized and that could not be institutionalized without more effective patterns of social control. To pursue the fiscal point of view in depth would require that consuming units adjust their spending patterns voluntarily in conformity to national needs and changes in the business cycle to a much greater extent than is acceptable under existing norms—or even that they accept with a high degree of compliance a system of price control or goods rationing.

As Aubrey Jones, the British economist who served in key price control assignments under both the Labour and Conservative governments, concluded, the realities of the political process have required the application of elements from both perspectives.[6] But the existing decision-making process at the various levels in the economy has basic shortcomings for implementing effectively and coherently any set of policies to deal with increased productivity and the control of inflationary pressures.

For more effective decision making, the process of institution building requires that a broader, more responsible role be taken by the trade union movement. The trade unions must be transformed from narrow, self-interested pressure groups into more responsible agencies in the overall management of the economy.

---

[6]Aubrey Jones, *The New Inflation: The Politics of Prices and Incomes* (London: Deutsch, 1973).

(The same perspective must be applied to alter comprehensively the role of the industrial corporation, but the basic issues can be illustrated by the trade union.) More effective social control rests on expanding the trade union's participation in decision making to produce more responsible results. In the United States and even in Great Britain, efforts to develop new legal norms for collective bargaining have been of limited consequence. Moreover, the state no longer possesses sufficient coercive authority to force the rank and file of strategic trade unions to comply with directives that their leaders reject. For example, in Great Britain in 1975, it was openly acknowledged that the military forces of Her Majesty's Government could not keep the ports open during a dockers' strike, nor could they man the power stations during an industrial shutdown. They certainly could not "dig coal with bayonets."

The restructuring of participation of the trade union movement in economic decision making involves both plant- and industry-wide levels plus national economic-level arrangements. There is every reason to believe that the system of social control of industrial–trade union relations in West Germany (and in Sweden as well) accounts for the lower ratio of inflation and for the higher levels of productivity. Institution building involves the development of a United States version of the German system of codetermination—a poor and misleading translation for *Mitbestimmung*, which really implies an element of participation and consent. It must be emphasized that German industrial relations contribute to the much lower level of official and wildcat strikes and to the more restricted level of inflation. In the United States, the adversary basis of labor relations, derived in part from a legal format, does not serve as a basis for effective national economic decision making. In the United States, it appears essential that there be an increased level of involvement at the plant level as the precondition for more effective participation in negotiating at the industry-wide or national economic level.

In the United States, at the plant level, the procedures are grounded in legalistic adversary relations concerned mainly with grievances that are supposed to be mediated by contractual and outside arbitration. This approach, which does not emphasize collective problem solving, has reached its limits. There is a sufficient body of experience to develop policy and experimental plant-level trade union participation that would be concerned with increasing productivity and dealing with worker dissatisfaction, absenteeism, poor work quality, and industrial sabotage, which are widespread in the United States. There is no need to offer utopian models, but the Swedish experiments in heavy industry indicate the potentials for teamwork groups, job rotation, and job enlargement.[7] Most important, they point to the positive contribution of worker consultation to collective problem solving as an alternative to an emphasis on industrial grievance procedures. These forms of worker participation do not

---

[7]Adequate research studies are not available. However, field reports indicate impressive reduction in turnover in specific cases from 50 percent per year to 20 percent per year, with noteworthy increases in productivity—for example, *The Wall Street Journal,* October 25, 1974. There is good reason to believe that some form of guaranteed annual wage is required to restructure employment in particularly heavily populated industrial settings if worker participation is to be effective.

imply basic changes in property rights but rather involvement in decision making as it concerns production based on negotiated economic incentives for increased productivity. Alterations of the conditions of work and the style of management to deal with the intangibles of self-respect and the quality of work emerge in these efforts with increasing significance. Worker participation in plant-level social welfare schemes is also a feasible goal. In this process, worker representatives may serve on the boards of directors with specifically designated authority.

Participation in plant-level decision making is an aspect of institution building for effective responsibility in negotiations at the industry level. Again, Germany (and Sweden) supplies a pointed case of more effective labor-management negotiations at the regional and national levels. Clearly, there are historical and cultural background factors. German trade unions are deeply conscious of the inflation of the 1920s and concerned with avoiding the trends that led to the rise of National Socialism. But the crucial element is that because of the structure of responsibility and institutional control, trade unions bargain with a concern for the economic well-being of the larger system. By contrast, the demands of the trade unions in the United States have been inflationary to the extent that regular pay increments are unrelated to increases in productivity and unassociated with fundamental issues of distributive justice. There are also demands for compensation unrelated to skill levels, work conditions, and the like. The trade union contribution to inflationary pressures includes increasingly mechanical payment of minimum wages that serves to prevent the entrance of young persons into the labor market. Moreover, the creation of annual pay increments leads to both expectations and rigidities that complicate economic resource allocation and fiscal policy.

However, the process of negotiating at the industry level cannot be made more responsible and subject to social control, especially in its implication for social welfare, without more institutionalized involvement of trade unions in formulating the national economic policy. In the United States, national economic allocation proceeds with a missing institutional link. Intense industrial collective bargaining operates without even informal linkage to national goals. There is no arrangement for formulating desirable goals for industrial and trade union enterprise while collective bargaining processes continue. Likewise, the federal government develops its budgetary allocations without explicit articulation with the pattern of industrial collective bargaining.

An institutionalization of a "summit" for national economic policy must be developed comparable to that implemented in countries like the Netherlands and, more implicitly, West Germany. The formation of a summit structure would have to be evolved outside of the structure of congressional decision making but closely related to it. In 1974, the Congress modernized its budget-making procedures in a more comprehensive and integrated format, which is more compatible with a summit conference for national policy. President Gerald Ford's national conferences on the economy, although viewed with skepticism by experts, can be regarded as first steps in this direction. It is noteworthy that the labor movement has responded by organizing its own national conference arrangements and indicating its acceptance of joint national economic discussion. There is a clear recognition of the need for national guidelines but only a faint initiative toward creating new agencies of social control of this variety.

The composition of the summit on national policy would stress participation by industrial and trade union representatives and spokesmen selected from voluntary associations on behalf of the public interest. The role of the experts would be advisory.[8] The goal would be to formulate national guidelines of economic targets for productivity and investment by exploring areas of agreement and disagreement. Social welfare objectives would become part of national bargaining. The targets would include alternative estimates of the supply of economic resources for social welfare as well as of the demand for welfare services.

The summit for national economic policy would

---

[8]The national economic summit would be supported by a permanent Office of National Economic Planning, attached to the highest level of the federal executive branch. The basic task of the agency would be to prepare short-term (three- to five-year) economic goals and plans, as well as long-term (ten- to fifteen-year) objectives. These materials would be designed for discussion and debate by the President and by the Congress. These planning documents would be advisory and would supply guidelines for administrative and legislative action. They would become elements in industry-labor collective bargaining and social welfare summits.

It should be noted that the United States government already spends about $200 million annually in basic economic statistics collection. It has been recommended, even by laissez faire economists, that the sum should be doubled; the collection of these additional data would be an essential component of these economic planning functions.

supply the essential forum for implementing a shift in the conception of welfare—away from its categorical definitions, which have created the sharp distinction between welfare recipients and the rest of the citizenry. The emphasis would be on a graduated system of payments designed to articulate with the realities of welfare needs as they are distributed throughout the social structure. In the area of income maintenance, the key is assistance to the working poor—the negative income tax or, as it is being relabeled, ABLE (Allowance for Basic Living Expenses). The criteria of functional assistance and the deemphasis of categorical assistance extend beyond income maintenance to all forms of social welfare, from assistance for post-high school education to medical care and the like. The guidelines that would be debated at the summit on national policy would be designed to improve the basis of labor-management negotiation regarding the capital investment required to maintain economic growth. The summit would clarify the choices that need to be made between competing welfare programs. Such an annual undertaking would be designed as an intermediate mechanism of social control with the purpose of strengthening and not supplanting the legislative process.

New goals in national income policy are gradually emerging. Crude measures of income equality are not sufficient from a research perspective. Likewise, to speak of the goal of "redistribution of income" or of "equalization of income" is much too crude from a policy point of view. In terms of effective social control, it is essential to establish an acceptable minimum family income, which can be achieved by an appropriate combination of negative income taxes, family allowances, unemployment insurance, and related programs. The elimination of the socially disruptive regulations against payments to families with working members is of course central. The present regulations produce corruption and demoralization as well as unmeasured economic waste.

Obviously minimum income objectives are more easily formulated than income policies for upper-income groups. It has come to be recognized that there are clear limits as to the level of taxation, especially of earned income, if appropriate incentives are to be maintained for professional and various categories of entrepreneurial personnel. At the level of the top 5 percent of earned income, it may well be the case that there is a level of direct taxes that inhibits work incentives and distorts economic productivity.

But this issue is different from that of unearned income accumulation. Inheritance taxes can be formulated for unearned income accumulation which permit the social control of excessive family fortunes without undermining financial incentives to invest in economic development. The standards are partly economic and partly sociopolitical for a society that emphasizes individual achievement. The "guts" of a tax policy involve the broad band of middle-income wage earners, and the issue is not only the amount of the family tax bill but the mix between direct income taxes and indirect taxes. There is good reason to believe that the problems of the welfare state are complicated by a heavy emphasis on direct income taxes, even if steeply graduated. This form of taxation is considered less legitimate by the citizenry than one that balances direct taxes with indirect taxes, such as sales and value-added taxation. Moreover, the overriding issue of tax legitimacy requires a system that is relatively simple in principle and that can therefore be more readily understood.

Transformation of Welfare Institutions

A vast amount of polemical literature has been written that voices the day-to-day criticism of and discontent with contemporary practices of welfare institutions. The demands for community control, which reached a high point at the end of the 1960s, symbolize the need for restructuring welfare agencies. Operationally, "community control" was in part a campaign to obtain municipal, state, and federal employment. It was also a demand for increased effectiveness and improved quality of welfare services. From the perspective of social control, at least three different elements were involved.

The first element was that the excessive fragmentation and specialization in welfare service need to be overcome. Bureaucratic jurisdictions hardly articulate with social requirements. Second, the improvement of welfare services should involve an increased emphasis on labor-intensive approaches rather than capital-intensive procedures. (Labor-intensive procedures include an increase in assistance in the development of self-help, while capital-intensive services in welfare include investments in professional education.) Third, the issues of improved accountability and of priorities were involved in the original demands for community control.

Moreover, there was and there remains implicit in these demands a search for the format by which welfare services can contribute to the individual's social and psychological integration into industrial society. The structure of welfare services at this point involves the psychological and therapeutic strategies discussed below. In a very profound sense, the word "community" was as important as the element of control. The welfare state, especially in the United States, had emerged with the strong imprint of a bureaucratic organization insufficiently concerned with the elements of community, of social cohesion and group identity as they operate as welfare objectives. The demand for community control was an impulse to construct entities that would combine a geographic base with ethnic, racial, and religious, or just local, sentiments.

There can be no doubt that intense demands for community control were often pressed without consideration for technical and professional realities. In turn, professional specialists and political leaders were often unprepared realistically to examine and respond to these demands. But a process of social learning leading to more effective social control was generated. Local leaders who demanded community control transformed their goals into measured community participation. New political leaders emerged from the efforts of community organizations of the 1960s, and the new generation of professionals who were in academic

127

training during these years were more sympathetic to changed procedures. The literature is burdened with reports of failed experiments, but expanded and more realistic community and client participation has become a persistent new direction in social welfare.[9]

While the community participation movement has focused mainly on local organization, the issues involve metropolitan and national structures as well. The goal of citizen participation is to create a more appropriate balance between centralization and decentralization. Paradoxically, the expansion of local citizen participation requires or, rather, is facilitated by increased centralization in planning and resource allocation. Basically, the United States welfare system is highly fragmented in its structure, in its policy formulation, and in its resource allocation. In a pluralistic society, the distinction between public and private is essential, although the overwhelming weight rests on the public sector; private efforts are to be judged not by their magnitude but by their specific accomplishments, their innovativeness, and the standards that they set.

The linkages between public and private social welfare institutions require not only adaptations of both types of institutions at the local level but also

---

[9]See Morris Janowitz, *Institution Building in Urban Education*, (Chicago: University of Chicago Press, 1971).

There are of course important differences between educational and social welfare institutions in the balance between specialization and aggregation. Educational agencies have been organized to emphasize the elements of institutional specialization. In part, this reflects the nature of the educational task, especially the cognitive goals. By contrast, it can be argued that social welfare agencies contain to some degree built-in limitations against excessive specialization. The source of aggregation reflects the diffuseness of the tasks to be performed. There is a persistent professional perspective in social work that stresses deprofessionalization. To mention these points is not to overstate the case.

essential institution building at the national level. An arrangement comparable to the assembly of national economic policy could emerge from the tradition of White House conferences on welfare topics. These conferences in the past have emphasized programmatic objectives but have failed to address the issues of priorities and national economic allocations. In the period of low productivity and chronic governmental deficits, the matter of an institutional format for welfare services emerges as central for national debate. There is no single conceptual direction for guiding the reconstruction of the organization of social welfare services locally or nationally. The extreme degree of institutional fragmentation and the operating code of rendering services on a highly specialized basis, which does not necessarily articulate with personal and social needs, must be overcome. Most generally, as has been described in regard to public education, the existing approach is that of "specialization": the development of highly trained specialists and particularistic agencies, which suffer from a lack of coordination and whose influence is limited because of their excessive reliance on capital-intensive procedures.[10] The opposite approach may well be called the "aggregation" emphasis. This goal stresses integration of services and reliance on labor-intensive approaches. Under these conditions, the social welfare agent would become a manager of a variety of resources in order to confront on a broader basis the needs of individual clients and social groupings.

One central strategy for overcoming fragmentation

---

[10]Ibid. *passim.*

and overspecialization is to regroup agencies operating in a common geographical area. In a residential community, this would provide the organizational structure for the fusion of highly specialized agencies and for more effective access. The geographic dimension is also designed to contribute to a sense of group cohesion and social solidarity of the citizenry involved, to inhibit excessive segregation of welfare recipients, and to facilitate the institutional base for citizen participation.

Contemporary welfare service agencies in the public sector tend to be organized along functional lines. Institution building requires that emphasis be shifted to a local community structure with some means of accommodating the requirements of functional specialization that do not articulate with a local community base. Thus, for example, the specialized services and complex intervention of vocational rehabilitation would operate on a functional base. No doubt the requirement of serving particular age groups creates pressures for specialized agencies, but, from the point of view of effective social control, the common geographic basis should inhibit excessive social segregation.

The emphasis on a geographic base in a community context for social welfare agencies is fully compatible with a continuation of a viable private sector in social welfare organized on a religious, ethnic, or even local basis. Private welfare agencies are designed to perform services that public agencies are unable to perform, to maintain higher standards of performance, and to carry out experimental programs. As such, private sectors can maintain a specialized agency structure and develop their own pattern of local community organization or relate closely to emerging public agencies.

At the local level, the school system, broadly defined, can be offered as the physical and functional center for restructuring social welfare services. Of course, there is a powerful argument against such institution building—the school system in the United States is already heavily burdened in its admixture of academic and socialization goals. To relate the public school more directly to the agencies of social welfare would burden it further and hinder it from accomplishing its central goals of academic and vocational preparation. However, the public school system, especially in the central cities, already suffers from overburdening, but that is because of the ineffective articulation between education and social welfare. Improved linkages between public education and the welfare system would result in an overall process of "debureaucratization"—if there is such a term.

Of the public agencies, the public school system touches the lives of most residents of the community. With the contemporary expansion of the definition of education to include adult education, the scope of contacts of the school systems within the local community expands. The school system, if only because of the aspirations of both parents and children, continues to have the greatest legitimacy of all the public agencies in the low-income communities as well. The pattern of articulation between education and welfare agencies would vary, depending on the type of community and the services to be rendered. The mechanisms range from the mere physical locale of specific services linked to income-maintenance programs to integrated services dealing with family education and community development programs.

The aggregation of specialized functions of social welfare services depends on new directions in the recruitment and training of personnel. At the core are the professional schools that train educational, welfare, and health specialists. There is little likelihood of any fundamental restructuring of the division of labor among these institutions. In fact, at the professional level the division of labor does represent distinct professional skills that need to be maintained. All three professional areas have common elements that could be taught on a common basis. Moreover, integrated professional training programs are required that assist the practitioner in dealing with activities that overlap the specialties.

Given the goal of emphasizing labor-intensive strategies, the aggregation function of linking the internal elements of social welfare and of fusing social wealth with health and education services should be implemented by paraprofessional personnel and by a strong emphasis on self-help. Self-help implies the use of clients, ex-clients, and local community personnel.[11] The design for recruiting, training, and using such personnel is gradually being developed. However, the central element is some form of voluntary national service—a concept that has been growing at the community and metropolitan levels but that requires organizational resources and policy at the na-

---

[11]Arthur Pearl and Frank Riessman, *New Careers for the Poor: The Non-Professional in Human Service* (New York: The Free Press, 1965).

tional level. The strength of a national voluntary service rests on its ability to recruit young people of high school and college age as short-term, highly motivated personnel who are prepared to undertake a range of essential tasks that cannot be purchased readily through the mechanisms of the marketplace.

A social welfare service system with a local community base, articulated with health and education functions by the use of labor-intensive personnel, can create the basis for meaningful citizen participation. The available literature demonstrates clearly that community organizations that are general-purpose, or even those with multiple functions, can play a role but face profound problems. Such organizations reflect specific local patterns of leadership but are often unstable and face difficulties because they tend to be incorporated into organized partisan politics. Instead, the "frontier" in citizen participation rests on the specific-purpose local voluntary association and on the direct involvement of local citizens in directing and administering particular social welfare agencies. The realities of a specific agency operate to create the potentials and limits of citizen involvement. The goals are pointed: to assist in establishing priorities, to increase the legitimacy of the agency, and to contribute to developing standards of performance. It is impossible to formulate highly generalized guidelines that are more than ideological slogans. But the dilemmas of the welfare state and the search for more effective social control are generating an expansion of citizen participation at the community level.

Psychological Intervention

Psychological intervention as an aspect of social welfare has a long tradition. Within the social welfare movement in both Great Britain and the United States, as two examples, there has been a strong emphasis on personal improvement—personal construction, if you will. In the nineteenth century, the recommended approach for personal construction included various types of group experiments that had religious and cultural roots as well as a psychological outlook. As indicated above, the welfare state need not be thought of as arising out of economic determinism, although the mechanisms of national accounts have become indispensable as a basis for the conceptual analysis of the difficulties of the welfare state. To an important degree, the origins of the welfare state may be considered as a response to the issues inherent in the frustrations of consumerism of an advanced industrial society. The alteration of the material conditions of life would not necessarily create a mortal order or human happiness.

In the United States, social welfare institutions have developed with strong overtones of an explicit psychological rationale. As mentioned above, the two men who had the most influence, Sigmund Freud and John Dewey, had a strong element of convergence in their efforts to reduce psychological misery and improve human morality. For them, the control of aggression—personal aggression and social aggression—was the central objective. They both evolved a body of thought which states that activist and rationalist ideas could enhance psychological potentialities if the fusion of the emotional and the rational components of the human being were recognized.

Support for psychological-based programs in the United States has been extensive but hardly at the level recommended by advocates of these approaches. There is scant evidence that the goals of programs—such as individual treatment casework, group work, community psychiatry, institutional treatment, and the variety of athletic, social, cultural, and artistic participation programs linked to social work—have been achieved. Nevertheless the goals remain with persistent and powerful tenacity. The continuing rationalistic or relativistic attack on "mental health" has not diverted the efforts of the committed specialists, reduced the demand for their services, or eliminated the social problem regarding mental health.

The forms of personal construction as well as treatment and therapy reflect the social structure. Under parliamentary regimes, it has been possible to create agencies for humane psychological support and assistance.[12] Human misery under advanced industrial society would have been greater without the variety of psychological practices that social work has engendered. Despite their limitations, defects, and distortions, their effect has been a contribution to standards of interpersonal behavior and a press for human decency. The prison psychiatrist was a beneficial public

---

[12]Barbara Wooton, *Testament for Social Science: An Essay in the Application of Scientific Method to Human Problems* (London: Allen and Unwin, 1950).

presence long before the courts took notice of the internal practices of custodial institutions. Caseworkers, even with an overload of clients, not only serve as informal ombudsmen but also offer an element of psychological support and human contact with the larger society. The introduction of treatment programs in youth correctional institutions has demonstrably made the milieu at least benign.[13]

Nevertheless, one can formulate an impressive list of failures of the welfare movement in its efforts on a psychological level—whether the programs be those of enlarging community involvement or of making explicit efforts at psychological intervention. First, in application, the conceptual basis has often been narrow and mechanistic. No doubt this derives from the tendency of psychological orientations to become orthodoxies. The influence of Freudian dynamic psychology on casework is an example. Efforts at pragmatic adaptation come very slowly. Second, under the stress of social tension and conflict, social welfare schools have overreacted and become critical of the psychological dimensions of the welfare state. Schools of social work, particularly in the late 1960s, had fadlike impulses, denounced therapeutic goals, and thought for a short time that they were launching a platform for political groups and partisan politics. This anti-intraceptive mood has subsided, but not without its residues of disruption and intellectual confusion. Third, the demand for psychological services has far

---

[13]David Street, Robert Vinter, and Charles Perrow, *Organization for Treatment: A Comparative Study of Institutions for Delinquents* (New York: The Free Press, 1966).

exceeded the ability of the society to supply them, especially since the institutions of social welfare have emphasized high capital (high human capital) investment. The efforts to modify the delivery of these services by means of a labor-intensive approach have brought about some progress, but much remains to be accomplished.

Given the limited capacities of the organized "helping" professions, it is understandable that under conditions of ineffective social control there has been a widespread and perhaps temporary diffusion of regressive therapies—from encounter groups, to physical manipulation, to extreme forms of behavior modification. But it would be an error to assume that more extensive social welfare institutions could have prevented the rise of these "therapies." It is more pertinent to require social welfare specialists to provide a consistent critique of such procedures and to maintain access to more standard services for those who are in need.

From a psychological perspective, social control and the institutions of self-regulation in an advanced society require the widespread development of persons who have strong personal control over their aggressive proclivities. There is also need for cadres of persons who have the tolerance and capacity for extensive and stable participation in a variety of group formations. No doubt in order to contribute to personal construction and redefinition of the therapeutic, social welfare institutions will require the continued development of specialized personnel and specialized agencies. But this aspect of institutional building is of secondary importance. The central issue is the psychological effect of the existing institutions of social welfare. Social workers speak of the overriding negative consequences of the stigma of welfare.[14] The shift from charity to welfare to income maintenance is but the symbolic manifestation of this preoccupation. More accurately, the issue is whether the benefits and services of social welfare institutions operate to segregate psychologically the recipients from the larger society or serve to link them, in one form or another, effectively to the social organization of the mass society. Each element for the reconstruction of welfare agencies discussed should at least mitigate presumed negative psychological impact. But citizen participation in the management of social welfare institutions is an integral aspect of the issues of participation in the management of stagflation. In essence, we are dealing with fundamental issues of authority relations and patterns of social control that operate generally throughout a society but that must take on forms appropriate to each particular institutional section. Each specific mechanism of effective social control relieves an overburdened political system and strengthens its effectiveness.

---

[14]See Robert Pinker, *Social Theory and Social Policy* (London: Heinemann, 1971), pp. 135–175.

Epilogue

IX: My exploration of the dilemmas
of the welfare state conforms to the sociological mode
of institutional analysis. There is an alternative approach, which must at least be acknowledged for the
sake of completeness. It is essential to consider the
character of the political elites in the United States,
since they have fashioned the welfare state. If one
wishes to close the gap between social research and
public policy, the issues of ineffective social control of
the welfare state cannot be limited to the impersonal
struggles and competition among the institutional sectors of an advanced industrialized society. Such a
perspective is much too overdetermined as to outcome. The dilemmas of the welfare state in the United
States reflect the limitations of the skill and leadership
style of the political elites, which are the crucial aspects of the elite structure.

The role of the political leaders is epitomized by the
failure of the Congress and the President to effect important reforms in the welfare system, exemplified in
the system of payments for dependent children. Only a
focus on the mechanisms of political management can
explain this failure. As early as 1960, with the election
of President John F. Kennedy, it was obvious that
major changes in this aspect of the welfare system
were necessary. In the next decade, a growing body of
research literature showed the disruptive effects of the

existing system of payments. The mass media generated extensive debate, and congressional leaders came to recognize the need to reform and modernize a system that weakened the structure of low-income families, especially of minority-group families. Throughout the Kennedy and Johnson administrations' period of extensive experimentation in social welfare, no fundamental effort was made to produce the required changes. During the first term of Richard M. Nixon, the Republican administration offered comprehensive proposals for altering the payment system, which included reform of the payments for dependent children. These reforms, articulated by Patrick Moynihan, stimulated counterproposals by Democratic party leaders and New Deal welfare specialists. However, the result of the intense debate was a stalemate—not even a limited piecemeal reform. The failure of the competing political leaders to articulate the national interest was clear. As of November, 1974, with the publication of the report entitled *Income Security for Americans: Recommendations of the Public Welfare Study,* prepared by Representative Martha Griffiths, a leading proponent of reform, the inertia about reforming welfare payments continued.[1] The deadlock of political leadership on this central issue reflected the lack of political initiative to confront the recession and the profound problems of allocating governmental expenditures.

Most students of welfare practices agree that exist-

---

[1] U.S. Congress, Joint Economic Committee, Subcommittee on Fiscal Policy, *Income Security for Americans: Recommendations of the Public Welfare Study* (Washington, D.C.: U.S. Government Printing Office, 1974). Epilogue.

ing policies denying family assistance payments to households with working males have served to create extensive patterns of cheating. (This is not to deny that welfare cheating has various origins, including bureaucratic inefficiencies.[2]) The socially destructive consequences of these procedures have been repeatedly emphasized.

It is difficult to explain the failure of political leaders to reform these requirements. It must be the case that these regulations serve some deep-seated social and psychological needs of the larger society. In the nineteenth century, the recipients of charity were defined as morally unworthy. One cannot dismiss the explanation that in the current setting such attitudes are still very strong in the larger society. The regulations that lead welfare families to "cheat" serve to perpetuate the image that the recipients of welfare continue to be morally unworthy. The rules and regulations operate to sustain the prejudices of the "respectable" elements of society.

This essay on the social control of the welfare state rests on the assumption that calculated self-interest—expressed in economic categories and economic goals—is at the center of political style and political participation in the United States but that such an orientation—at the levels of the elites and of the citizenry—is not sufficient to generate a system of effective self-regulation of competing societal interests.

---

[2]See U.S. Department of Health, Education, and Welfare, Social and Rehabilitation Service, Division of Quality Control Managements, *Quality Control in AFDC: National Findings, January–June 1974 Reporting Period* (Washington, D.C.: Department of Health, Education, and Welfare, March 1975), mimeographed.

The notion of effective governance is not merely moralistic but is also a central aspect of the processes and mechanisms of social control. Governance—and its content of responsibility—rests on the standards and behavior of the economic, political, and cultural elites, regardless of the degree of diffusion of power and authority. All that has been argued in the analysis of the institutions of the welfare state cannot divert attention from a direct focus on elite groups and the conditions and elements involved in influencing their behavior.

In the simplest terms, the vast United States educational system, the structure of the political parties, and the context of social and moral values have not operated in recent decades to develop cadres of political leaders with the levels of skill and responsibility to the larger political community that are required for appropriate and effective social control. The leadership of key institutional sectors reflects the mode of those particular political leaders with whom they must interact and, therefore, contributes in turn to the short-term and particularistic outlook of important segments of the political elites. The parliamentary systems of the West during this period of intense internal strain operate because a minority of elected officials have the ability to separate themselves from the ongoing process of political decision making. These leaders demonstrate highly personalistic characteristics or have strong political resources. In addition, there seems to be an institutional explanation for the emergence of these prime movers in the elected political arena.

The division of labor in political competition and in

day-to-day legislative work affords the opportunity for a limited number of men and women to emerge as leaders. In a democracy, it is as if the impact of history—past and present—were exerting a positive effect. Ascent to higher office is a gradual and long-term process. Examination of the "natural history" of political recruitment affords only the most limited optimism. Paradoxically, a parliamentary regime involves extensive opportunity for the circulation of its elites, which is both a source of weakness and a potential for change. Even more important, it may well be that in a mass democracy with the complex tasks of the welfare state, the emergence of more effective middle-level political leaders—as well as more effective middle-level institutional managers—is both the essential requirement and the more likely prospect.

It was in the 1930s that Harold D. Lasswell, the political scientist and political sociologist, drawing on the writings of Pareto, Mosca, and Michels, emphasized the intellectual task of examining the behavior of elites as part of a comprehensive study of the processes of sociopolitical change.[3] He documented the broadening of the social base of recruitment of professional and elite groups—a trend that may be called the "democratization of recruitment" of elite groups. He spoke of the middle-income skill revolution. But he was fully aware that the democratization of social recruitment of professional and elite groups did not ensure effective performance or guarantee a

---

[3]Harold D. Lasswell, *Politics: Who Gets What, When, and How* (New York: Meridian Books, 1958); Lasswell, *World Politics and Personal Insecurity* (New York: The Free Press, 1965).

strengthening of their sense of responsibility in governing the welfare state.

Unlike Great Britain, the United States has not been subject to rule by an entrenched "establishment," narrowly recruited from the upper strata and educated in a very limited number of uniform institutions; yet the demands for broadening the base of social recruitment of professional and elite groups have been politically pervasive in the United States and extensively supported by intellectuals and by university and college teaching personnel. Clearly, an important degree of representativeness is required in the elites of a democratic polity. The exclusion of particular minority groups from political leadership has obviously weakened the patterns of social control in the United States. It is even more difficult to argue that a restriction or a narrowing of the base of recruitment would have increased the elites' performance. The crucial formulation is that with increased industrialization and a more complicated division of labor, social origins serve less and less as indicators of elite behavior; instead, the processes of socialization—educational, community, and career—emerge as more central dimensions.

Harold D. Lasswell's writing did stimulate an increased interest in the empirical study and analysis of elites and elite behavior. A great deal of this energy has been expended in the specific debate about pluralistic versus monolithic power structures. Fundamental analysis of the processes of recruitment and socialization of the moral character of the elites—and their relevance for effective social control—has not been sufficiently confronted. Moreover, there is little intellectual ferment in university centers about these fundamental issues.

Nevertheless, one sociological observation stands out: for a political elite in a parliamentary system to operate effectively and to govern responsibly, its members must share some values that contribute to their concern with the larger political community. These common values are likely to be rooted in shared experiences. The absence of a feudal tradition, the social heterogeneity of the nation, and intense political populism have inhibited the emergence of a political stratum.

This is not to overlook the fact that despite populistic traditions the "upper class"—more accurately, the upper stratum of inherited wealth—for better or for worse have contributed heavily to the ranks of the political elites. However, the broadening of the social base of recruitment into the political elites that has been progressively at work since the middle of the nineteenth century has meant a relative decline in the proportion of persons from the upper socioeconomic stratum among those in active political careers. The traditions of upper-class political leaders have been under continuous attack in the United States and have in fact been attenuated over the long run.

More and more, it has been university educational experience rather than social position that has propelled men into political careers and engendered concern with the larger political community—to the extent that such concerns are operative. (In fact, that minority of the political elite that is still drawn from the upper stratum reflects family tradition less and the influence of university education and the events of career experience more.) Available documentation has probed the effect of legal training and the opportunities of a legal career that have supplied the essential stimuli for the cadres from which the political elites have been overwhelmingly drawn.[4] It is interesting that, proportionately, the less prestigious law schools have served to develop interests in political careers. Their contributions have, in the past, been crucial in recruiting people for the informal, diffuse political careers that lead to higher elected office in the United States. It is also important that family tradition has been strong in influencing young men—and now young women—from modest social backgrounds to enter these law schools and then embark on political careers.

Likewise, for better or for worse, since 1920, military service has supplied an essential ingredient and a common experience for those seeking elected office. "Military service" implies service not as a professional officer but as a citizen-soldier during a national emergency or for a short tour of duty. Military service has operated at least to develop notions of responsibility to the larger political collectivity. Available documentation indicates that military service has not produced a strong emphasis on hawkish attitudes in foreign policy.[5] If anything, it has served to strengthen

---

[4]Donald Mathews, *United States Senators and Their World* (New York: Random House, 1960); Heinz Eulau and John D. Sprague, *Lawyers in Politics: A Study in Professional Convergence* (Indianapolis, Ind.: Bobbs-Merrill, 1964); Heinz Eulau and Kenneth Prewitt, *Labyrinths of Democracy: Adaptations, Linkages, Representation and Politics in Urban Politics* (Indianapolis, Ind.: Bobbs-Merrill, 1973).

[5]John N. Colas, "A Preliminary Examination of the Influences of Military Background on Legislative Behavior: Some Indications from the 88th U.S. Congress" (Unpublished manuscript, University of Chicago, Inter-University Seminar on Armed Forces and Society Archives, 1966).

interest in the government's role in welfare. Collective problem solving during wartime serves to strengthen the belief in governmental intervention. Military service has been a device enabling men from minority groups to enter the political arena. Military service has generated a broader view of the larger society and a stronger commitment to the political community and has implanted in many the aspiration and idea of a political career.

However, with the broadening of the social basis of recruitment, the proportion of political leaders with legal backgrounds and the importance of the common experience of legal training have started to decline. Furthermore, the influence of military service in fashioning political leaders is also being attenuated. The war in Vietnam has hardly been an integrating experience, and the concept of the citizen-soldier is rapidly declining with the end of the mass armed force and conscription. Even in the absence of systematic data, there is evidence that the agitations of the civil rights movement and of the student movement of the 1960s have thrown up new cadres from which political leaders are being drawn. In general, one must acknowledge that the fragmentation of elite socialization and the diversification of political career lines continue. The United States university system has marked limitations in supplying the range of intellectual and social experiences required to develop new cadres from which the political elites will be drawn. The sheer size and diversity of the university system limit its capacity to educate for leadership. Clearly, the ambivalent attitudes of the faculties toward organized politics— especially the sociology and political science faculties—are a crucial factor. The faculties of the United States university system are unable to think of themselves as performing an essential educational role by training political leaders.

Thus, it is understandable that in order to strengthen social control of the political process a series of legalistic procedures are being debated and implemented that are designed to improve the quality of political leadership. First, there are efforts to develop codes of ethics for elected officials. The main direction of these efforts is to explicate procedures for dealing with conflicts of interest and to require elected officials to disclose sources of personal income. Second, legislative efforts are being made to control more comprehensively the procedures and financing of elections. These efforts also involve limiting campaign expenditures and transforming or at least shifting the base of campaign funding from private donations to support from public sources. No doubt many of these reforms are desirable because among other consequences they are likely in and of themselves to increase the legitimacy of the electoral system. However, there is no reason to assume that governmentalized campaign funding—one of the key reforms—will decisively increase the effectiveness and responsibility of the elected political elites. There is the strong possibility that this reform will isolate the political leaders from public pressure and decrease their accountability. If it has merit, it is that it will decrease the strain involved in postelection fund raising, especially for defeated candidates. The long-term consequences include, potentially, decreasing the very high rates of turnover among emerging political leaders and increasing their longevity in the political arena whether they win or lose. Such a trend would be very desirable, since it would strengthen the knowledgeability, skill, and group cohesion of active political cadres.

But these legal and administrative efforts at social control hardly appear adequate to encompass the tasks of a political elite that must seek to resolve sharply competing social and political claims and the attendant tensions and conflicts. It is not moralistic to be concerned with building institutions to improve the quality of the political leaders who must be concerned with the problems of the welfare state. The education, socialization, and career experiences of the political elites of parliamentary political systems seem to constitute a set of problems that even defy formulation, let alone systematic, constructive institution building. The issues involve not only the potential elected political leaders but also the broad range of political leaders for special interest groups, who are responsible for presenting and defining the substantive and fiscal matters of social welfare.

The democratization of recruitment and the diversity of elite careers are the given realities of a parliamentary democracy and in fact the requisites of a democratic polity. Thus, in effect, we are not dealing with nineteenth-century concepts of elite education and socialization, designed for very specific and delimited groups, including a handful of promising representatives from the submerged strata. Instead, we are dealing with "citizenship education" in the broad sense of the term, which involves significant segments of the social structure and diverse groups of political activists.

Academics have argued that one key is the drastic improvement in academic instruction in the social sciences, especially in political science and economics, to clarify the essential issues in the social control of the welfare state. But clearly more than the intellectual function of higher education is involved. The teachers of social science have an ambivalent and unstable set of values about political leadership, and their concern with higher education as a moral enterprise has yet to be adequately articulated and implemented. This is not to denigrate the range of imaginative experiments in clinical and apprenticeship training that innovative faculty members in certain institutions offer their students in community and political participation. These efforts, when they are successful, have an intellectual element and do not politicize the college or university involved.

With the end of the eruptions of student protest in the 1960s, a new reappraisal of the position of both high school and college education in United States society came into being, if only because of fiscal stringency. There has been increased debate and discussion of alternative pathways into adulthood in the search for a new admixture of academic and work experience. Educational reform in the United States often takes the direction of single-dimension social movements. There was, in recent history, a concern with the acceleration of cognitive learning as the central issue, according to one group of specialists; another group focused on preschool education. There was a period in recent history when racial desegregation was viewed as the key approach to the improvement of educational performance.

I hope that work-study programs will not be offered as a comprehensive solution to the very complex problems of citizenship training in advanced education. With the end of conscription, the United States has rejected the notion of voluntary national service—the trauma of Vietnam was too great for such an approach to citizenship education and the socialization of new leadership groups. However, the range and diversity of local and particularistic experiments in community and public service that have been launched since the end of the United States intervention in Indochina are striking. Until these experiments are given a logic and a purpose related to national goals, they will at best have only limited influence, mainly as a strategy for helping individuals adjust to the existing system of higher education. But even these small-scale experiments provide important opportunities for citizenship training in the complexities and dilemmas of social welfare. Clearly, extensive programs for directly involving high school and college students in the procedures and mechanics of community and political organizations are essential mechanisms of citizenship training in a democracy. If we are moving toward public subsidy of campaign funds, it could be that public subsidy of community and political apprenticeship is the next step, although there are strong reasons for organizing such experiments in citizenship training on a nongovernmental basis.

Existing educational institutions are only partially

effective and appropriate loci for such strategies of citizenship education. Nor can the emphasis be limited to young people seeking to enter the labor market. Citizenship education encompasses different stages in the life cycle. In essence, we are seeking "lateral" entry into various levels of political leadership.

I have argued that effective social control of the welfare state rests on an extensive but realistic broadening of the basis of citizenship participation in the management of local community and metropolitan institutions. This requirement supplies varied opportunities for on-the-job leadership socialization and citizenship education throughout various phases in the life cycle of a still very small but significant segment of the adult population. Many, if not most, experiments in citizenship participation are strained by the quality of local leadership and by the lack of opportunity for training and developing the competence of the participants. However, we must be venturesome and make use of these new opportunities for recruiting leadership and for judging the commitment and effectiveness of new cadres of activists. In the United States, nonpartisan organizations have traditionally supplied a crucial base for recruiting political leadership. The new dimension is the extensive increase and the broadening of the base of opportunity that the welfare state generates. There is no alternative, since academic components of citizenship training, even augmented by imaginative civic apprenticeship or "group dynamics" experiments, cannot substitute for the realities of civic participation with real responsibility. Moreover, citizen participation in extraparliamentary institutions will, it is hoped, serve to strengthen the effectiveness of periodic national elections, but such participation can hardly substitute for the basic mechanism of social and political control. In the language of Joseph Schumpeter, the effective competitive election has been and remains the hallmark of a political democracy.

Acknowledgments

This essay is a portion of my larger study on macrosociology and social control. I wish to acknowledge the generous assistance of the Russell Sage Foundation, which made it possible for me to write on this subject. In particular, I wish to thank Orville Brim, Jr., and Eleanor Bernert Sheldon, who as foundation executives supported this type of research. I wish also to express my appreciation to the previous "generation" at Russell Sage Foundation, Donald Young and Leonard S. Cottrell, Jr., men whose sociological imagination and leadership fashioned that foundation into an innovative center of social research.

I was able to write this study because of the intellectual discourse and colleague support that are at work in the "reconstituted" Department of Sociology at the University of Chicago. Of course, this setting is a reflection of the academic enterprise in the Division of the Social Sciences of the University of Chicago. It would be beside the point to acknowledge the help of particular persons, although some of my colleagues were more sympathetic than others. But I would like to acknowledge the particularly helpful criticism of William Wilson. I would also like to acknowledge the assistance of Shelley Abelson and James Bone in completing this manuscript.

A group of lifelong intimate colleagues with whom I

attended graduate school have been indispensable in fashioning my views about macrosociology: Albert Biderman, Otis Dudley Duncan, Albert J. Reiss, Jr., Ralph Turner, Guy Swanson, and Harold Wilensky. Over the course of years, I have had continuing intellectual assistance from both Allan Silver and Mayer Zald as well. Specific stimuli for this essay derive from three associates with strong interests in the issues of social welfare—Robert Vinter, Dave Street, and Jerry Suttles—who have sought to supply a counterweight to chronic generalizations.

The act of writing this essay was made possible by the presence of Lloyd A. Fallers.

Bibliography

Aaron, Henry J. "Social Security: International Comparisons." In Otto Eckstein, ed., *Studies in the Economics of Income Maintenance*. Washington, D.C.: The Brookings Institution, 1967.

Abrahamson, Julia. *A Neighborhood Finds Itself*. New York: Harper and Bros., 1959.

Abrams, Mark. "Political Parties and the Polls." In Paul F. Lazarsfeld, William H. Sewell, and Harold L. Wilensky, eds., *The Uses of Sociology*. New York: Basic Books, 1967, pp. 427–436.

Abrams, Philip, ed. *The Origins of British Sociology, 1834–1914*. Chicago: University of Chicago Press, 1968.

Anderson, Odin W. *Health Care: Can There Be Equity?— The United States, Sweden, and England*. New York: Wiley, 1972.

Back, Kurt W. *Beyond Words: The Story of Sensitivity Training and the Encounter Movement*. New York: Russell Sage Foundation, 1973.

Baker, Keith. *Condorcet*. Chicago: University of Chicago Press, 1975.

Becker, Howard. *Outsiders: Studies in the Sociology of Deviance*. New York: The Free Press of Glencoe, 1963.

Bettelheim, Bruno and Morris Janowitz. *Social Change and Prejudice*. New York: The Free Press, 1975.

Bradburn, Norman and David Caplovitz. *Reports on Happiness: A Pilot Study of Behavior Related to Mental Health*. Chicago: Aldine, 1965.

Briggs, Asa. "The Welfare State in Historical Perspective." *Archives of European Sociology,* XI (1961): 221–258.

Brown, Norman O. *Life against Death: The Psychoanalytical Meaning of History.* Middletown, Conn.: Wesleyan University Press, 1959.

Bruner, Jerome. *The Process of Education.* Cambridge, Mass.: Harvard University Press, 1960.

Burnham, W. D. "The Changing Shape of the American Political Universe." *American Political Science Review,* LIV (March 1965): 7–28.

————. *Critical Elections and the Mainsprings of American Politics.* New York: Norton, 1970.

Colas, John N. "A Preliminary Examination of the Influences of Military Background on Legislative Behavior: Some Indications from the 88th U.S. Congress." Unpublished manuscript. University of Chicago: Inter-University Seminar on Armed Forces and Society Archives, 1966.

Cole, Richard L. *Citizen Participation in the Urban Policy Process.* Lexington, Mass.: Lexington Books, 1974.

Coleman, James S., et al. *Youth: Transition to Adulthood: Report of the Panel on Youth of the President's Science Advisory Committee.* Chicago: University of Chicago Press, 1974.

Commager, Henry Steele, ed. *Lester Ward and the Welfare State.* Indianapolis, Ind.: Bobbs-Merrill, 1967.

Converse, Philip E. "Change in the American Electorate." In Angus Campbell and Philip E. Converse, eds., *The Human Meaning of Social Change.* New York: Russell Sage Foundation, 1972, pp. 263–338.

Coser, Lewis A. "Max Weber, 1864-1920," *Masters of Sociological Thought.* New York: Harcourt Brace, 1971, pp. 217–260.

Dahl, Robert. *A Preface to Democratic Theory.* Chicago: University of Chicago Press, 1956.

Dahrendorf, Ralf. *Class and Class Conflict in Industrial Society.* Stanford: Stanford University Press, 1959.

David, Paul T. *Party Strength in the United States, 1872-1970.* Charlottesville, Va.: University Press of Virginia, 1972.

de Grazia, Alfred and Ted Gurr. *American Welfare.* New York: New York University Press, 1962.

Dewey, John. *The Public and Its Problems.* New York: H. Holt, 1927.

Dicey, A. V. *Lectures on the Relation between Law and Public Opinion in England during the Nineteenth Century.* London: Macmillan, 1930.

Downs, Anthony. *Urban Problems and Prospects.* Chicago: Markham, 1970.

Durkheim, Emile. *Le Suicide.* Paris: F. Alcan, 1897.

Duverger, Maurice. *Political Parties: Their Organization and Activity in the Modern State.* New York: J. Wiley, 1959.

Eulau, Heinz and Kenneth Prewitt. *Labyrinths of Democracy: Adaptations, Linkages, Representation and Politics in Urban Politics.* Indianapolis, Ind.: Bobbs-Merrill, 1973.

Eulau, Heinz and John D. Sprague. *Lawyers in Politics: A Study in Professional Convergence.* Indianapolis, Ind.: Bobbs-Merrill, 1964.

Fallers, Lloyd A. *Inequality: Social Stratification Reconsidered.* Chicago: University of Chicago Press, 1973.

Faris, Robert E. L. *Chicago Sociology: 1920–1932.* Chicago: University of Chicago Press, 1970.

Fraser, Derek. *The Evolution of the British Welfare State: A History of Social Policy since the Industrial Revolution.* London: Macmillan, 1973.

Freud, Sigmund. *Psychopathology of Everyday Life.* New York: Macmillan Co., 1914.

———, trans. C. J. M. Hubback. *Beyond the Pleasure Principle.* London: The International Psycho-analytical Press, 1922.

———. *Introductory Lectures on Psychoanalysis.* London: Allen and Unwin, 1922. .

————, trans. Jean Riviere. *Civilization and Its Discontents*. New York: J. Cape and H. Smith, 1930.

Friedmann, Georges. *Industrial Society: The Emergence of the Human Problems of Automation*. Glencoe, Ill.: The Free Press, 1955.

Galenson, Walter. "Social Security and Economic Development: A Quantitative Approach." *Industrial and Labor Relations Review*, XXI (June 1968): 559–569.

Gordon, Margaret S. *The Economics of Welfare Policies*. New York: Columbia University Press, 1963.

Gray, Alexander. *The Socialist Tradition: Moses to Lenin*. New York: Longmans Green, 1946.

Greenstone, John D. and Paul Peterson. *Race and Authority in Urban Politics: Community Participation and the War on Poverty*. New York: Russell Sage Foundation, 1973.

Hamilton, Richard F. *Class and Politics in the United States*. New York: Wiley, 1972.

Hillman, Arthur, ed. *Making Democracy Work: A Study of Neighborhood Organization*. New York: National Federation of Settlements and Neighborhood Centers, 1968.

Hollister, Robert M., Bernard Kramer, and Seymour Bellin. *Neighborhood Health Centers: What Do Demonstration Projects Demonstrate?* Lexington, Mass.: Lexington Books, 1974.

Horkheimer, Max. *Eclipse of Reason*. New York: Oxford University Press, 1947.

Hurwitz, Samuel J. *State Intervention in Great Britain: A Study of Economic Control and Social Response, 1914–1919*. New York: Columbia University Press, 1949.

Janowitz, Morris, ed. *W. I. Thomas, On Social Organization and Social Personality*. Chicago: University of Chicago Press, 1966.

————. *Political Conflict: Essays in Political Sociology*. Chicago: Quadrangle Books, 1970.

————. *Institution Building in Urban Education*. Chicago: University of Chicago Press, 1971.

———. "Volunteer Armed Forces and Military Purpose." *Foreign Affairs,* L (April 1972): 428–443.

———. "Social Control and Sociological Theory." *American Journal of Sociology,* LXXXI (July 1975): 82–108.

Janowitz, Morris and Dwaine Marvick. *Competitive Pressure and Democratic Consent.* Chicago: Quadrangle Books, 1964.

Johnson, Harry. *On Economics and Society.* Chicago: University of Chicago Press, 1975.

Jones, Aubrey. *The New Inflation: The Politics of Prices and Incomes.* London: Deutsch, 1973.

Kallen, David and Dorothy Miller. "Public Attitudes toward Welfare." *Social Work,* XVI (July 1971): 83–90.

Key, V. O., Jr. "A Theory of Critical Elections." *Journal of Politics,* XVII (February 1955): 3–18.

Kirchheimer, Otto. "The Waning of Opposition in Parliamentary Regimes." *Social Research,* XXIV (Summer 1957): 117–156.

———. "Confining Conditions and Revolutionary Breakthroughs." *American Political Science Review,* LIX (December 1965): 964–974.

Kobrin, Solomon. "The Chicago Area Project—a 25 Year Assessment." *Annuals of the American Academy of Political and Social Science,* CCCXXII (March 1959): 19–29.

Lane, Robert E. "The Politics of Consensus in an Age of Affluence." *American Political Science Review,* LIX (December 1965): 874–895.

Lasswell, Harold. *Democracy through Public Opinion.* Menasha, Wis.: George Banta, 1941.

———. *Politics: Who Gets What, When, and How.* New York: Meridian Books, 1958.

———. *World Politics and Personal Insecurity.* New York: The Free Press, 1965.

Lieberson, Stanley. "An Empirical Study of Military-

Industrial Linkages." *American Journal of Sociology,* LXX (January 1971): 562–584.

Lipset, Seymour M. "The Changing Class Structure and Contemporary European Politics." *Daedalus,* XCIII (Winter 1964): 271–303.

———— and Earl Raab. *The Politics of Unreason: Right-Wing Extremism in America, 1890–1970.* New York: Harper and Row, 1970.

Long, Norton E. "The Local Community as an Ecology of Games." *American Journal of Sociology,* LXIV (September 1958): 251–261.

Lubove, Roy. *The Professional Altruist: The Emergence of Social Work as a Career, 1880–1930.* Cambridge, Mass.: Harvard University Press, 1965.

Lynd, Robert S. *Knowledge for What? The Place of Social Science in American Culture.* Princeton, N.J.: Princeton University Press, 1939.

Mannheim, Karl. *Man and Society in an Age of Reconstruction.* London: Kegan Paul, 1940.

Marcuse, Herbert. *Eros and Civilization: A Philosophical Inquiry into Freud.* New York: Vintage Books, 1955.

Marris, Peter and Marlin Rein. *Dilemmas of Social Reform: Poverty and Community Action in the United States.* New York: Atherton Press, 1967.

Marshall, T. H. *Citizenship and Social Class.* Cambridge, Eng.: University of Cambridge Press, 1950.

————. *Class, Citizenship, and Social Development.* Garden City, N.Y.: Doubleday, 1964.

Marwick, Arthur. *Britain in the Century of Total War: War, Peace, and Social Change, 1900–1967.* Boston: Little, Brown, 1968.

Marx, Karl. *Capital: A Critique of Political Economy.* New York: The Modern Library, 1936.

Mathews, Donald. *United States Senators and Their World.* New York: Random House, 1960.

161

McGranahan, Donald V. "Social Planning and Social Security." Bulletin No. 7. Geneva: International Institute of Labour Studies (1970).

McMillen, Neil R. *The Citizens' Council: Organized Resistance to the Second Reconstruction, 1954–1964*. Urbana: University of Illinois Press, 1971.

Miller, Herman. *Income Distribution in the United States*. Washington, D.C.: Department of Commerce, Bureau of the Census, 1966.

———. *Rich Man, Poor Man: The Distribution of Income in America*. New York: Thomas Y. Crowell, 1971.

Miller, S. M. and Pamela Roby. *The Future of Inequality*. New York: Basic Books, 1970.

Miller, Walter B. "The Impact of a 'Total-Community' Delinquency Control Project." *Social Problems,* X (Fall 1962): 168–191.

Moore, Barrington, Jr. "Revolution in America." *New York Review of Books,* XII (January 30, 1969): 6–12.

———. *Reflections on the Causes of Human Misery and upon Certain Proposals to Eliminate Them*. Boston: Beacon Press, 1972.

Moynihan, Daniel P. *Maximum Feasible Misunderstanding: Community Action in the War on Poverty*. New York: The Free Press, 1969.

Murphy, Thomas P. *Services to the Neighborhood*. Lexington, Mass.: Lexington Books, 1974.

Myrdal, Gunnar. *Beyond the Welfare State*. New Haven, Conn.: Yale University Press, 1960.

Neumann, Franz. *Behemoth, the Structure and Practice of National Socialism, 1933–1944*. New York: Octagon Books, 1963.

Park, Robert E. and Ernest W. Burgess. *Introduction to the Science of Sociology*. Chicago: University of Chicago Press, 1921.

Peacock, Alan T. and Jack Wiseman. *The Growth of Public Expenditure in the United Kingdom*. Princeton, N.J.: Princeton University Press, 1961.

Pearl, Arthur and Frank Riessman. *New Careers for the Poor: The Non-Professional in Human Service*. New York: The Free Press, 1965.

Pechman, Joseph A. "The Distributional Effects of Public Higher Education in California," *The Journal of Human Resources*, V (Summer 1970): 361–370.

Pechman, Joseph A., Henry J. Aaron, and Michael K. Taussig. *Social Security: Perspectives for Reform*. Washington, D.C.: The Brookings Institution, 1968.

Pinker, Robert. *Social Theory and Social Policy*. London: Heinemann, 1971.

President's Research Committee on Social Trends. *Recent Social Trends in the United States*, I and II. New York: McGraw-Hill, 1933.

Pryor, Frederick. *Public Expenditures in Communist and Capitalist Nations*. London: Allen and Unwin, 1968.

Reiss, Albert, Jr. "Delinquency as the Failure of Personal and Social Control." *American Sociological Review*, XVI (April 1951): 196–207.

————, Otis D. Duncan, Paul K. Hatt, and Cecil C. North. *Occupations and Social Status*. Glencoe, Ill.: The Free Press, 1962.

Reynolds, Morgan and Eugene Smolensky. "The Post F I S C Distribution: 1961 and 1970 Compared." *National Tax Journal*, XXVII (No. 4): 515–530.

Riessman, Frank, Jerome Cohen, and Arthur Pearl, eds. *Mental Health of the Poor*. New York: The Free Press of Glencoe, 1964.

Rimlinger, G. *Welfare Policy and Industrialization in Europe, America, and Russia*. New York: Wiley, 1971.

Ruggles, Richard and Nancy D. Ruggles. *National Income Accounts and Income Analysis*. New York: McGraw-Hill, 1956.

Runciman, W. G. *Relative Deprivation and Social Justice: A Study of Attitudes to Social Inequality in Twentieth-Century England*. Berkeley, Calif.: University of California Press, 1966.

Russett, Bruce. *What Price Vigilance? The Burdens of National Defense*. New Haven, Conn.: Yale University Press, 1970.

Sabine, George H. *A History of Political Theory*. New York: H. Holt, 1937.

Sahlein, William. *A Neighborhood Solution to the Social Services Dilemma*. Lexington, Mass.: Lexington Books, 1974.

Schiltz, Michael A. *Public Attitudes toward Social Security, 1935–1965*. Research Report No. 33. Washington, D.C.: Social Security Administration, Office of Research and Statistics, 1970.

Schultz, Theodore W. *Investment in Human Capital: The Role of Education and of Research*. New York: The Free Press, 1971.

Schumpeter, Joseph. *Capitalism, Socialism, and Democracy*. New York: Harper and Bros., 1942.

Shils, Edward A. "The Theory of the Mass Society." *Diogenes*, No. 39 (1962): 45–66.

Spergel, Irving A., ed. *Community Organization: Studies in Constraint*. Beverly Hills, Calif.: Sage Publications, 1972.

Steiner, Gilbert Y. *The State of Welfare*. Washington, D.C.: The Brookings Institution, 1971.

Sternlieb, George S. and Bernard P. Indik. *The Ecology of Welfare: Housing and the Welfare Crisis in New York City*. New Brunswick, N.J.: Transaction Books, 1973.

Street, David ed. *Innovations in Mass Education*. New York: Wiley-Interscience, 1969.

Street, David, Robert Vinter, and Charles Perrow. *Organization for Treatment: A Comparative Study of Institutions for Delinquents*. New York: The Free Press, 1966.

Suttles, Jerry. *The Social Order of the Slum*. Chicago: University of Chicago Press, 1968.

Titmuss, Richard. *Essays on the Welfare State*. London: Allen and Unwin, 1958.

Turner, Ralph H. *On Social Control and Collective Behavior*. Chicago: University of Chicago Press, 1967.

W. E. Upjohn Institute for Employment Research. *Work in America: Report of a Special Task Force to the Secretary of Health, Education, and Welfare*. Cambridge, Mass.: The MIT Press, 1973.

U.S. Congress, Joint Economic Committee, Subcommittee on Fiscal Policy. *Income Security for Americans: Recommendations of the Public Welfare Study*. Washington, D.C.: U.S. Government Printing Office, 1974.

U.S. Department of Health, Education, and Welfare, Social and Rehabilitation Service, Division of Quality Control Managements. *Quality Control in AFDC: National Findings, January-June 1974 Reporting Period*. Washington, D.C.: March 1975. Mimeographed.

Warren, Roland. *The Community in America*. Chicago: Rand McNally, 1963.

Weber, Max. "Der Sinn der 'Wertfreiheit' der soziologischen und ökonomischen Wissenschaften." *Logos*, II (1917).

————, trans. Edward A. Shils and Henry A. Finch. *On the Methodology of the Social Sciences*. Glencoe, Ill.: The Free Press, 1949.

————, trans. A. M. Henderson and Talcott Parsons. *The Theory of Social and Economic Organization*. New York: Oxford Press, 1964, pp. 329–341.

————, trans. Edward A. Shils. *On Universities*. Chicago: University of Chicago Press, 1974.

Wilensky, Harold. "Mass Society and Mass Culture: Interdependence or Independence?" *American Sociological Review*, XXIX (April 1964): 173–197.

———— and Charles N. Lebeaux. *Industrial Society and Social Welfare*. New York: Russell Sage Foundation, 1965.

————. *The Welfare State and Equality: Structural and Ideological Roots of Public Expenditures*. Berkeley, Calif.: University of California Press, 1975.

Wilson, William. *Power, Racism and Privilege: Race Relations in Theoretical and Sociohistorical Perspectives*. New York: Macmillan, 1973.

Wooton, Barbara. *Testament for Social Science: An Essay in the Application of Scientific Method to Human Problems*. London: Allen and Unwin, 1950.

Wrigley, E. A. "The Process of Modernization and the Industrial Revolution in England." *Journal of Interdisciplinary History*, III (Autumn 1922): 225–259.

Zald, Mayer N. "Sociology and Community Organization Practice." In Mayer N. Zald, ed., *Organizing for Community Welfare*. Chicago: Quadrangle Books, 1967, pp. 27–61.

Index

167